UNDER THE
SIGN OF THE
LABYRINTH

Under the Sign of the Labyrinth

CHRISTINA TUDOR-SIDERI

A SUBLUNARY OBJECT

ISBN 978-1-7349766-0-1
Library of Congress Control Number: 2020943281

First edition. Second printing.

Manufactured in the United States of America
Printed on acid-free paper
First published by Sublunary Editions in 2020
Design and typesetting by Joshua Rothes
Cover image "Ariadne" by Jackson/Singer, taken from *La Grèce
pittoresque et historique* by Christopher Wordsworth, Paris, L. Cur-
mer, 1841.

Sublunary Editions
Seattle, WA
sublunaryeditions.com

Contents

Under the Sign of the Labyrinth

The wound is past all cure. Just as when in a watered garden, if someone should break off violets or stiff poppies or lilies, bristling with yellow stamens, fainting they suddenly droop their withered heads and can no longer stand erect, but gaze, with tops bowed low, upon the earth.

—Ovid, *Metamorphoses*, Book X

She needs to tear God apart; for against God, who is the end, the outcome above all others, she asserts herself as refusal, refusal to ever accept an alien end. And she needs the torn-apart God who is the labyrinth—and against the labyrinth she affirms her free movement, her ability to unfetter herself.

—Maurice Blanchot, *On Nietzsche's Side*

I

ANAMNESIS

Trauma lives in the body. It lives in the body of all things—past, present, and future. Yet to write of trauma is to write of the nature of an eternal and interiorized present. To write of trauma is to crawl back into the wilderness of your soul like an animal wounded by humans crawls back into the forest. To write of trauma is to walk a path that requires a certain setting provided by your memory as it struggles to preserve the self—your memory, positioning itself at the intersection of ruin and allegory. To write of trauma is to throw yourself against the wall with the strength of waves clashing against one another during the most tempestuous of nights. In *Remedia Amoris*, Ovid writes of learning to heal from the one who has taught us how to love—"one hand alike will wound and succor." Modifying the body and organs of memory, archiving the past, recording and sometimes rearranging your history; all become necessary to the writing act. The tales, thoughts, experiences, and memories that live inside myself segregate my history into two distinct entities: one of motor mechanisms, the other of independent recollections. The history that resides within me speaks not only of actions that have happened once, in the distant past, it speaks of actions that have repeated themselves to the point of erasure. The history that resides within me speaks of trees, rivers, wounds, hands.

Searching through those archives for voices, thoughts, and memories that can help me piece together the story of a beginning I can live with, I stumble upon an idea from one of the philosophy journals I used to keep under the bed as a child. A particular passage comes to mind, as my fingers trace the imaginary rubble—a passage discussing humans and animals and what tells them apart in relation to intentional behavior. I brush it aside for a second, yet it weighs on me still, so I allow it to invade my mind: If we were to look at the differences between humans and animals in terms of voluntary choices, we would see that they are not as pronounced as we'd expect. The distinction is one of degree, rather than one of nature. An animal can memorize the movements of its body, turning them into images that later assist it in the execution of intentional actions. As do humans. Similarly, animals are able to perfect this process with the help of their experiences, such as avoiding an action that causes them pain, regardless of the external impetus to perform it. Yet we consider the acts of humans the result of free will, while we think that animals lack this ability. Animals and humans make use of the same primordial mechanism—it is the degree to which we improve that mechanism that tells us apart. It was in those same journals that I read the line, "we cannot know for sure if all humans who live in nature are mortals,"—words that have amused, comforted, and tormented me throughout the years. Nature is intentionally seeking to bring together all contrasts, and it is due to this endeavor that we strive for perception beyond any and all subjective elements of affection and memory. It is due to the processes of nature that we seek to interpret experience as instant vision, as pure perception— something that is not as much a part of the spirit as it is a part of the environment that makes us humans.

Growing up, I was guided—albeit tenderly—by a curious set of concepts and beliefs that were ever-changing and yet never strayed from the mythical nature serving as their foundation. Rocked to sleep by loving hands, poems, fairy tales, fables, and stories, variations of *the primitive I* revealed themselves to me in emotions and sympathies that, as an adult, I drifted away from. My grandmother used to tell me that people are sensitive to emotions such as rage, pride, or possession long before they become sensitive to nature, light, or color. A sort of narrow anthropomorphism, if one were to consider the beliefs of the elders about how we are not born human, but rather progress into our humanity as life passes. I remember closing my eyes and seeing the blue sea caressing the sand—as blue as the sky with which it blended perfectly at the horizon. The water was calm. There were no clouds, there was no sacred calling, there were no recollections of the forest asylums that would later shape my understanding of a disturbed sense of living in the world. As I was rocked to sleep, tales helped me fall soothingly into dreams that often aligned with thoughts of travelers who, exhausted from the road, dreamed of resting, if only for a moment. To write of trauma is to dig through hours and hours of family history—beliefs, dreams, disorders—searching for shades and variations of transgenerational trauma, an array of fears and emotions that have always escaped me. To write of trauma is to revisit the beautiful moments. The moments caressed by the rudimentary beauty of the small village where I spent the first seven years of my life, the moments when November poured its coldness into my soul, the moments when, later in life, I could no longer hear the river whispering its sagas.

I decide to take a walk to the train tracks. There is no station, there is nowhere to go, nothing to do but watch the trains pass by as their shadows become one with the canopy of the forest. As my steps travel the narrow path, I think of how death takes pleasure in tormenting the nameless. Death, with its limpid eyes and scarred face, it too a shadow, trailing the fleeting trains—engulfing in its breathless sigh all souls of the nameless. Seconds later, I am staring at a dot on the ceiling. The moon spills its cool over poppy fields. Years pass, and my thoughts carry me back to the graves of the nameless. They carry me back to stories I wrote, to the magical amaranthine color of the

pink

sky at dusk over the cemetery every time there was a fire nearby. I think of magic—experimental metaphysics. I think of magic and how I cannot forget the elm trees that cover the ground where the mundane meets the grotesque, where humans and mythical creatures alike bow their heads, honoring their deities. I think of magic, and I am a child again. I crawl under the bed and am transported inside my memories, inside what should have been my own history. I see a film showing the miniature world I used to live in—frame after frame of sunrises on the valley, midnights under linden trees, caresses, lullabies, tales, hunger, rain, beasts, televised massacres. I see them stone-cold and somber, like statues belonging in a Resnais film, deriving pleasure from the mathematical precision of their carefully curated frames. I move my eyes to guide the auditorium, but I soon forget and submerge myself wholly into the story. I fold my arms under the bed, a way to make sure I will not leave the frame before the film ends. I take the shape of the doorbell from a memory of earth trembling. People are kissing the ground in front of their homes. I feel the sun on my skin, which must mean it's the middle of the afternoon, yet I am swiftly reminded that I am still indoors by the sound of my grandparents' pill bottles falling from the television set. A voice calls me outside. I do not want to leave the house, so my grandmother comes in—I know it's her because I recognize the sound the door makes when her hand opens it. She tries to pick me up but I start screaming and tell her I want to stay inside where I am safe. Pausing to recapture the meaning of those words, I realize that although I had no understanding of safety at that age, I had lied to her, for I did not care about the earthquake, nor about feeling safeguarded under the roof of our house. What I wanted was to keep drawing flowers on the faces inside the pages of my books. As objects and framed memories keep falling around us, she grabs me by the hand, hoping I will allow her to pick me up. Time moves more slowly than usual. A picture from my first day in kindergarten falls inside a bucket with water we were keeping for the plants. My mother's high-school photo falls on the bed and then on the floor, causing the glass to break. A row of dolls neatly aligned on top of the bed frame tumble down at the same time as two Russian fairy tale books that stood on the improvised nightstand. She drags me outside, and as she rushes to the street, the gravel scrapes my knees. Rose thorns cling to my skin. She does not stop walking, I do not stop protesting, the earth does not stop trembling. Eventually, I say I am sorry, kiss her hand, and ask to be carried. She cries and returns the kiss, tending to my injured knees. It has happened before. My mother as a young girl studying in a nearby city, alone as a violent earthquake brought down almost all buildings. It has happened before, which is why my grandmother struggled to protect me regardless of my protests. We are all in the street. Neighbors, cats, dogs, the boy who likes me, ducks, parents, grandparents, a frightened mouse seeking shelter away from humans, the girl to whom I gave my beloved doll in exchange for a book with pictures of communist leaders from around the world. I drew flowers on their faces. I am four years old. Later in the afternoon, I am sitting with my grandmother under the fig trees. She is reading me a poem about a Romanian soldier who missed his train home and was killed in battle the next morning.

I grow up, and the memory becomes a film frame. It becomes a line in my journal, a cicatrix on my wrist, a word on my body. Memories thriving on their nonlinearity. Another frame. I am inside the house of a stranger. I close my eyes; this time I can run away. What I am searching for is not in this world. It is not in the world crumbling around me, nor in the history that embodies new meaning after new meaning each time I revisit it. To write of trauma is to negotiate the boundaries of life, whether it is a life hidebound by rules or the overabundance of a tree swinging the silence of the world on its branches. Some civilizations believed that the form of a city can influence the lives of its inhabitants. Others, that tidal forces are responsible for life and death. When clouds turn red at dusk, the wind will blow violently the next day. Dwelling on unravelling the mysteries behind experiences, superstitions, observations, magic, myth, the memory of folklore, and the anamnesis of collective life will tighten the rope of time. Each word becomes a scream. Starving trains pass by my window with the heaviness of a dark eternity that cannot be erased once I travel back in search of what wounded me. Light becomes diseased. The genesis of poetry is expunged. Pain has a momentum of its own yet again, unceremoniously slouching within the hollow and cold urn that entombs it. There are times when I know the location of my pain with such precision that if someone were to put a scalpel in my hand, I could excise it down to the very last cell without harming any healthy tissue. Thereafter, the blade whets itself. At other times, my acquiescence to the demands of pain and trauma cloaks me inside my own nature. Not of human, not of animal—the nature of a being who throbs in harmony with the passing of time. So I search inside my mind and the minds of those around me. I search for voices, memories, thoughts—anamnesis.

I was sixteen the first time I heard a voice inside my head. I remember the words as if I were hearing them now in the rustling of falling city leaves, yet that is not relevant in helping me search for the root I long to pluck from the earth that raised me. It was not the message it carried that made me choose the path I chose. Those words did not map my future steps. It was its immediate departure that governed my thoughts for years to come. Feeling deserted by my own insanity, while not yet sane. Absence. It was not difficult to search for it. It was not difficult to put myself in situations that would require the presence of a voice inside my head. I searched for it in books, on forest trails, in music, in the sounds of the sea, in the seams of the clothes I tore off when I felt that that was the only control I was bestowed with. I searched for it in the crushing heaviness of smoldering nights, and later, in the words I would write. Little by little, the search was replaced by my conviction that I could no longer hear it because it had shattered into a thousand other voices—right there, inside my mind. A thousand other voices that died at various times and in various places while traveling where they can be heard again. I liked that thought—it made me feel full. My body became the site of voices brought together after death: a thanato-coenosis of whispers and thoughts. Fragments that refused to reveal themselves to me, but which I was now steering to where they belonged with the very movements of my limbs. It occurred to me that reading might help my mind become a better vessel. Thus I began to hoard books and open them erratically at various hours of the night. I was reading about the eternal return, about the endless echoing of cosmic acts—about myths, history, patterns of the pre-Socratic man. Everything overwhelmingly unrelated to my search. "One must be familiar with all archaic ontologies," I would say to myself, mockingly, while smoking against the walls of some secluded bar. Unknowingly, I was setting little traps for the voice to return. I have always been good at capturing things with my mind. When I started seeing shapes, lines, and black dots out of the corner of my eye, I thought that I am finally getting my sign.

I remember reading in the philosophy journals under my bed something along the lines of: "if we were to study the behavior of the archaic man, we would be surprised by the fact that—much like human acts—the objects of the exterior world hold no value for him, not in themselves." It was then that I started touching everything. I would take objects into my hands—sometimes even kiss them gently—and hold them until they felt impregnated with symbolism. A mythical act of bringing all things into the reality that would later devour them. Other gestures gained different significances. Touching the hand of another became something so charged with meaning that I could no longer do it. It made me feel like a deserted island in the middle of a frozen landscape. It made me feel that I had failed in my quest to become the perfect vessel for an uprooted beginning. Not everything was gone. I felt something within me, still. I felt myself inhabited by monsters who never dared to show themselves, not even to me—the one feeding and keeping them warm.

That voice never returned, and its words faded with time. Perhaps the voices that I thought I transported inside me, the dead voices, perhaps they were the monsters with mighty teeth, gnawing at my flesh from within when I needed it the most. It was at around that time—in illo tempore, as the gospel taught me—that I abandoned my mother tongue, for I knew of no other way to retreat from language. I knew of no other way to walk in silence alongside the absence of all sound. I started writing what I would later call *interrupted manuscripts*, one for each time I needed the voice and it did not return. "You have been marked by Chronos," a folklore book chanted from my pile. To walk along a stream, with a dead poem in my head. I would come to know greater agonies.

We stop living in profane time when we take it upon ourselves to imitate a divine archetype, more so if we do it misguided by others. Mircea Eliade speaks of something similar throughout his work, yet in reference to the sexual act. But there, in the country of my childhood, those words meant living a life without sin. Without touch. Everywhere I went, I listened to the voices around me. I listened, I rebelled, I gathered all words and braided them in my hair to keep me company at night. My hands, however, felt more helpless than ever. All that my hands could gather would perish in an instant, in the same manner in which the voice perished—within the new, within the irreversible. Had I killed them? Had I suffocated all the voices with my smothering silence? As wounds started to heal, these thoughts grew distant. I found a way in which to disguise my true nature. I allowed others to decode and decipher me, for I knew they would find no real face. Thus occurred my break-up with the act of breathing meaning into lifeless objects. I began ridiculing the voices screaming at me from spineless books about the timeless space of primordialism and the paramount source of human behaviors—all the enlightened writers. Who were they to have a voice? And more crucially, how dared they waste it on such indecent doctrines? My life was no longer overshadowed by moments of doubt, I no longer needed the warmth brought by a voice in my head at sixteen. Delusion dictated my steps—the path ahead was glorious: sullied by the promise of death, yet exhilarating to walk on.

For a while, I survived like that. I survived with monsters inside me, for everything they would consume, I would breathe back on the bone the next day. A sublime process of wounding and healing—the world itself. I survived, for only a living body can be loved. Only a living body can be touched, caressed, smelled, gazed upon, tasted, heard. Only a living body can die. So I kept myself alive, not with the hope of ever hearing whatever voice I needed to hear—but because of its very absence. For its absence. I kept myself alive for the promise of distant death.

The world is now crumbling outside my reach. I am sensitive to nature, light, color. To write of trauma is to reopen all wounds—those that scarred you and those that didn't. To write of trauma is to devour yourself and never be full. To become your very own sin-eater. To feed on all that wounds you and all that heals you.

II

THE MAD FOREST

Wild men and women meander through the forest. They have been banished there by their kinsmen, left to fend for themselves, to become lawless—beasts and monsters traveling the paths of the woodland, released from the ideal of societal reason. They devote themselves to inbetweenness and to the construction of transient lodgings. Their disjointed and monstrous minds and bodies still torment and haunt the imagination of the towns and villages from which they were exiled. Deep into the heart of the old forests, wild men and women have abandoned all reason—as such, they are thought of as beings of terrible and incomprehensible proximity to nonhumanity. They are nonhumans.

One of the first shapes I learned how to draw was that of an uprooted tree—symbol for the woodlands surrounding our village. As a child walking the paths of the forest, I became fascinated by how people found use even for its leaves. If left in water, the leaves of wild apple trees together with those of withered marjoram give out a beautiful light red color, which we frequently used to dye wool threads. Walking through the woods, collecting leaves, I often wondered if people have always done this—if in the primordial forests, there were humans searching for color. In *A Treatise and Discourse of the Laws of the Forest*, John Manwood writes of the original forests, of their laws and outlaws, of afforestation and later the destruction that caused the birds and beasts to retreat into the sanctuary of what was left—of what constitutes a forest, "for many other places have woods, coverts, and fruitful pastures, yet are no forests." The memories I have of life at the outskirts of the village are often incomplete, hectic, or disappearing—yet there are times when they invade my mind as if they were the only memories I were allowed to keep, as if I were reliving the lives of everyone around me, family, neighbors, and strangers alike. As if I am reliving the olden days, when the boundaries of settlements were decided based on their position in relation to the woods. Studying old Romanian documents from around the 1400s, I found numerous references to such descriptions—"from the well, straight on to the high forest... from the white brook, upwards to the high forest..." I close my eyes and I envision myself rafting down the river and its tributaries, along the lines of the profuse wildwood—my fingers following the movement of clouds and birds in the air. I envision myself beyond the confines of the world.

Withdrawing from civic life, disrupting the alignment of daily habits, returning to a primordial state of wandering with an inner aim rather than governed by a collective one, provides us with camouflage and revelation—but it also changes our nature in the eyes of others. We become wild, lawless, uncontrollable. To walk around, to search for flowers, to dip your fingers into the crevasse of a wellspring, to locate freedom elsewhere than in the heart of a community—to become one with the nature that sheathes the spaces of your mind and protects the shape of your body, to descend into the definition of madness as established by those sane enough to speak in the name of all. To walk the line between human and nonhuman and thrive on getting lost rather than on returning to one's abode. To become animal.

Before 1882, when Robert Koch identified the causative agent of tuberculosis and published his findings—changing the way in which the medical community regarded the disease—sanatoriums and preventoriums for housing tuberculosis patients were being built all over Europe. As early as 1830, forests, due to their fresh air and secluded nature, provided ideal locations for such establishments. After his discovery, the sanatoriums that were once meant to offer comfort and treatment to patients were either abandoned—as was the case throughout but not limited to Eastern Europe—or transformed into mental asylums. Situated north from the Danube, the *Mad Forest*—its name originating from the Petcheneg-Cuman migratory populations that inhabited the land between 900 and 1240—housed a number of such sanatoriums within the vast woodlands that once covered the southwestern part of Walachia. By the time tuberculosis was being properly treated and sanatoriums were no longer needed, more and more communities took on the endeavor of exiling their mentally ill deep into the forests or along the banks of rivers.

Dressing the wound of a tree was strictly forbidden in the village, not only because there was no need for human intervention in the processes of nature, but also because the elders considered it an offense to judge a tree, a plant, or an animal for what it has endured. The most beautiful trees in the forest were those struck by lightning. Nature belonged to another realm, it represented the adventurous soul that human beings were not allowed to have—a soul that was not only celebrated, but also protected. The *Mad Forest* celebrated nature as well—its endurance, courage, and offerings. For nature was allowed to dwell in madness—it was allowed to create and thrive in its lunacy. It was also expected of nature to heal *our* lunacy. As time went by, asylums, one after the other, became worlds of their own, secluded from the rest of the community not just because of their location, but also due to the rules they governed themselves by. Disconnected from the world, prevented from participating in the day-to-day life and the development of its culture, the asylums took on the shape of their impending decay long before their walls started to show signs of erosion. As the medical personnel became less engaged, and as the people living in the towns and villages nearby started to forget of their existence, the inhabitants of the asylums granted themselves the freedom they were denied, roaming through the forests at will, making temporary dwellings under the protection of oaks, poplars, and acacias. The crossing of the bridge was no longer forbidden.

Wild men and women meander through the forest. They step into the river; they break out—even if only momentarily—from the shackles of time passing; they escape a time that transforms therapy into torture. Even though they may get lost and perish into the depths of its engrossing core, in the *Mad Forest*, wild men and women walk shoulder to shoulder, holding hands, searching for flowers.

> *This hospital, through its setting in the middle of the park, along the banks of the river, highlighted by a natural and most admirable beach, could become—with small sacrifices—a preventorium housing mentally ill children, predisposed to tuberculosis, from all over the province.*
>
> — Proposal to build a preventorium in a Romanian village. Written by the county doctor and published in the *Dimineața* (The Morning) newspaper, 1 December 1934.

My earliest memory is of running water. The village ambiance, stratified in the unstoppable love-of-life of a three-year-old child, in the unconscious mind and rural sonorities overlapping perfectly with acts of transcendence and the devouring nature of time. Beauty, cruelty, joyfulness. Running water. I am here alone, with waves rumbling at my feet and memories from years ago deepening the mystery of my inability to tolerate chronology. The Baltic Sea is the color of lead. Silvery, with a hint of blue, it places before me the drowning ashes of time, carving the fall from paradise on sand that I will never touch again. The sea, like lead, bonds with itself—it bonds with itself and the debris of wailing waves accumulates in my tissues and bones, damaging my nervous system in an all-too-necessary act of subjugation.

The hospital was built in 1937. Throughout the years, the children living there have left their mark on the village in ways that words could never capture. Sometimes I would see them before my eyes as silhouettes following the river downstream, resembling fairies dancing on therapeutic waters. At other times, my grandmother would tell me stories about those who survived, how they grew into adults behind the gates of the preventorium—stories of nocturnal escapes and beguiling adventures in the nearby forest. I would like to forget the here and now and remember myself on the banks of the river, surrounded by older children speaking to me of big city libraries and dreams of one day leaving the village. Instead, my mind travels to the first poem I ever learned to recite. "The coffins of lead were lying sound asleep…" I don't remember this myself, but my mother says I used to recite it accompanied by hand-and-body gestures that would make everyone feel uncomfortable. As the poem takes my mind further from the children I never met to years later playing under the murmuring of the same river, admiring the same red valley of poppies, getting lost at night in the same dark forest, my feet no longer feel the heaviness of waves. Amidst tall grass, the child discovers the world.

I often think of childhood as a state of pre-existence—not as Plato thought of humans carrying within themselves knowledge from some abstract world of ideas, nor as religious denomination, but as a collection of moments that fall under no reign. A mass that carries no discomfort within, a stasis of beautiful non-duration. And yet, one of the first lessons I was taught in early childhood was that all things carry immediate consequences, whether you are a child, an adult, a bird in flight, a healing wound, or a blade of grass caressing the stem of a neighboring flower. In our small village of eternal descent, the sacredness of one's own actions was believed to travel the body like indispensable poison—love of fate being its only antidote. Doodling under the lilac tree behind the house, I felt proud of being given the chance to learn such a lesson—since for me, my grandmother's words had nothing to do with being careful when climbing up high in the trees, with not getting lost in the forest or in the fields—nor did it mean never walking into the river by myself or to always keep a safelight on at night. Her words meant I had choices, and those choices would act as a map guiding me towards a forthcoming, towards a voice I would later recognize as my own. A crucial transition from lines, words, lilac fragrance, and innocent desires, to the cradle of my being. I spent my childhood ignoring most of what adults warned me about, yet I always made sure to know what my actions could do. And when I didn't, that *something* was still necessary, otherwise I would stop in the middle of a time-thrust, in the duration of an illusion, under the very same lilac tree where I first learned to tread not lightly but with sentience. I would stop and see the map erasing itself before my eyes.

Living in a small village made my life tenderly connected to the lives of everyone around me, from the blue-eyed boy two houses away to the spellbinding existence of preventorium nurses and doctors. I remember calling it the *fall into history* long before I ever discovered Romanian philosophers' predilection for the concept. For me, it meant being thrust into the same existence along with everyone else around—living or dead. A means for us to write our history, word by word, with unknown hands, collectively; to inhabit the flesh of the world as one: the heart of the village. In Romanian literature, and perhaps in that of other Eastern European countries, the village plays a crucial role in the development of the soul—its intricate structure becomes the foundation of everything from symbolism to philosophy, societal commonness, or morals. Building their houses around important landmarks such as the church, the hospital, the cemetery, the pharmacy, or the mill, countryfolk carry on with their existence in their own time, untouched, yet ruthlessly injured by the demands of the modern world.

"Eternity was born in the village," wrote poet and philosopher Lucian Blaga. My eternity dragged its mellifluous insides along the narrow paths of the forest, under the two bridges us children were always afraid to cross, behind hospital desks, around the bonfires of almost mythical midnights—all the way up to the attic of our house, where I would hide for hours to read, play with mice, or watch the sunset. Just as I carry within me a time when paradise was truly that—mouth-watering apples and luscious gardens—my eternity carries within itself the weight of the village, the bodies of its inhabitants, and the consequences of all our actions.

In the summer of 2005 I drove my car into a tree. I don't remember the exact date, but I like to believe that it was on the night of Saint John. *Sânziene* eve, when heavens open up, giving magical powers to those who seek love; bestowing health on the people and blessing the fields—robbing any man who lingers in watching the fairies of his voice or hearing and driving him insane. The forest smelled of linden blossoms. The narrow path through which you could drive deep into the heart of another time felt like an open highway. I was no longer a child, therefore I had stopped participating in midsummer night rituals—yet there I was, school break after school break, weekend after weekend, always returning home, with all of yesterday inside me. On the night of Saint John, or on any other night during which my grandmother would practice her white magic rituals, I would drive throughout the village, down the street to the church and the cemetery, then up to the gates of the preventorium, listening to cassettes of strangers reading the words of Cioran, Bacovia, Eliade, Kafka, or Baudelaire. A project that I had started in high-school back in Bucharest—recordings made by a secret book club. We would receive books from each other and send back cassettes of our readings—sometimes with grave accents, other times in unintentional bursts of laughter. I made sure that all the books were the ones I had read as a child living with my grandparents—a way to bring back pieces of my childhood into the grayness of a city I could never call home. Eleven years after starting school I was still furious with my parents for my very own fall from paradise. Reaching out of the car window, I threw what memory tells me was a disposable camera, as far as I could, without looking back to see where it landed. That was the moment when my hand either no longer wanted to or could not handle the wheel. There was no opening of the heavens, the air did not feel magical, and the sounds of the forest at night spoke of nothing but the forceful comprehension of my actions. My map was erasing itself. A few moments later, a deafening noise brought with it apparitions of 1940s children playing along the banks of the river.

The village's hospital was adjacent to the preventorium, separated by a tall fence and a small forest of cherry trees and acacias. Every trip there meant an opportunity to get a glimpse into the lives of its inhabitants and the medical personnel tending to their needs. Sometimes someone would slam a door so loudly that its sound traveled for minutes through the hallways of the small pediatric wing of what the villagers used to call *the good hospital*. For me, it was a secret reverie, proof that people were alive in there—that they were part of our village as much as the nurse who was getting ready to test my blood for signs of disease. The atmosphere felt burdened with everything that was left unsaid, too much for a child to understand, even in the truthfulness of life spent side by side with eternity and the serenity of not knowing what death is.

Outside the Berlin train station, I reach out my arm and offer its flesh to the rain. What I feel are not the feverish drops of a March cloudburst, but the touch of fabrics from long ago. I feel the linen of summer nights, the comfortable wool of winter mornings. I feel lace, silk, and embroideries that stay on my skin even after I am sound asleep next to my grandmother. When I finally allow myself to feel the raindrops on my skin, the time within speaks to me of holding the hand of a blue-eyed boy as we make our way into the old river. We are going on a mussel hunt. We have seen our grandfathers do it, and, although neither of us says a word, we are confident we can get it right. The sun is shining brightly, and as I look back to catch a glimpse of the rustling summer trees, I hear the older children screaming at us from the sandbanks. "Come back from there, you don't want to die before seeing the city, do you?" We turn, still holding hands, smiling mischievously as our eyes meet, knowing that such notions—*death* and *the city*—mean absolutely nothing to us. In that moment, there exists no rupture in the organic connection between our innocence and spending eternity in the village.

Many years later, walking upstream one evening, I

think about how inevitability alters its shape from one moment to another, about the primordial fear of those who felt they had lost themselves to the idea of the eternal village—a mythical expansion of reality. Visiting landscapes of my childhood positions me between nature as comfort zone—a respite from the hastiness of other places, other people, other times—and the disquiet of stepping on a ground now bereft of children unfamiliar with death. The village is as disarmingly humane as ever. The view is overwhelming—in the distance, the forest trees are humming spells about the flow of time and werewolves climbing to the moon. According to lunar-protection spells and other fragments of Romanian folklore, if a woman is spinning wool at night without candlelight, the wool thread will allow werewolves to climb to the moon and devour it, which is how fortune-tellers explain the blood moon phenomenon. Even in the presence of eternity's last breath, I cannot separate the beliefs of another life from the demands of space and time. I could always recognize the violence of being taken out of time—the surgical precision with which it excises all humans and possessions from existence. It is in moments like these that I allow it to foolishly speak to me of being timeless. At the edge of the village, close to the natural and most admirable beach, being thrown out of time is synonymous with being timeless. Here, the passage of time embraces you in much tender ways than in the city. Yet the wound with which it marks you cannot be healed, not even by the touch of unageing youth and deathless life. One final look back and the forest canopy tells me I have become the village itself—I am drawing the map encircling all the landmarks of my being. Walking back to the train station in the neighboring village, I carry within me this other time, I am providing a flawed shelter for an existence much too sane for the city lights to come.

The preventorium was closed by the authorities in 2011, prior to which it was turned into a senior living facility. I do not know what happened to the last of its inhabitants, nor if they were the same people I sometimes saw walking the streets of the village looking for someone to tell their story to. I have often dreamed of going beyond its gates, of walking along the narrow stream I could hear from the outside, of ripping apart the fairy tale books of my childhood and draining them of healing water to pour on the wounds of those inside. I have dreamed of finding someone I could speak to about my exhaustion, about the arms of time that embrace me and prevent me from falling, about our small village and how I felt that its soul was now residing behind the cemetery gates. Above ground, plucking flowers to place on discarded graves, I listen to George Enescu's *Childhood Impressions in D major*, a piece written one year after our preventorium was built. I feel its unaltered character crawling under my skin—not in the form of musical notes, but as a kaleidoscope of butterflies one does not have the heart to cast away. Tragedy transposed into music. What I should be doing is planting flowers, not plucking them, yet I can't get myself to dig into this soil, to have my bare hands touch the roots of these plants. It is as if the music is preventing me from doing so. There lies eternity, tossing and turning in a grave that was—is—undeniably unfit for casing its rotting flesh and graceful suffering.

The history of how my philosophical framework came into existence is a graveyard for all that *was not and will not be*. I have buried there all ideas, thoughts, and hypotheses that did not serve the purpose of uprooting myself, of always being in motion. Yet notwithstanding the direction I gave it, under the vivid light of the possible reigning over the real, the concepts that my mind uses in depicting itself as the thought that thinks the *being* or the subject that infiltrates the *object* dress themselves according to their needs. To find oneself before the real with the despair of the agnostic or the certainty of the gnostic is to think that the thirst for the primordial life and meaning of the word can be quenched as effortlessly as throwing a wet blanket over a small fire. Syllogism does not authenticate; it merely falsifies. I have seen mythical fires dying out and becoming water; I have seen the sea broken down by ethereal combustion. I have seen burning without flames and souls nourished by the disfigurement it brought. Behind masks, with their will strengthened by the anomalous. I have seen ceremonial fire—sometimes scattered and diffuse, other times as vigorous as Bacchic rage. I have been told about the purification of sinners by fire. The pretense of it. I have read about eternal flames engulfing the evils of humanity in writings carved by poets from the granite of words. I held my hand over a flame only to feel it as cold as ever. I have seen faces melted away by fire. In dreams, in nightmares, as apparitions before my eyes, in the faraway horizons of other lives. I have seen flesh succumbing to the ever living Heraclitic fire that kindles the world.

My great-grandfather built houses. On winter nights, when we were all gathered around the hearth baking apples or brewing tea, my grandmother would proudly tell us stories about the houses in the village and how most of them were built by her father. She had accompanied him as a little girl and even learned to lay bricks long before my great-grandmother taught her how to prepare a meal. It was one of her most fulfilling memories because girls of a similar age were kept at home and taught how to cook and do chores around the house while their grandfathers, fathers, and brothers were out building houses, ploughing the fields, or working at the mill. For me, the village was this magical place where one would discover all the wonders of nature, where you could get lost for hours in a game or running through the most beautiful landscapes. For my grandmother, it was always the place she could never escape. A borderless space that nevertheless lures and entraps one under its artificial dome. And thus, the memories of being a carefree child, walking hand in hand with her father to serve the noble purpose of building a home are the ones she always treasured most. One evening, the house dearest to him caught fire. He had worked on it during his first years as a builder. A small but striking abode, on the same street as ours. A house that I admired whenever I passed it on my way to the river or the forest. At the time, he was living at the other end of the village, confined to his bed, comforted solely by his newspapers and crossword puzzles. When I rushed over to his house to tell him about the incident, he said that in the heart of this land nothing ever happens without a reason and that the fire will bring our community together like a wound dealt to the body brings together all organs in order to heal. Like a crack in the walls of the church brings together all parishioners in order to fill it. As he said those words, he repeated my grandmother's name after each sentence, lovingly but with a sadness in his voice that I did not know how to interpret for many years to come. It made me painfully aware that I knew close to nothing of the man who, for a brief moment in my childhood, held my hand and taught me how to ride a bicycle. I would later search for him in all the faces of strangers whose gait resembled his.

Thinking about the interpretation of fire throughout history, I wonder whether the many meanings we assigned to it have led to the deconstruction of its significance since we connect the injuries one suffers from fire to such a wide array of beliefs. There is not only one type of injury and there is not only one type of intention. Burn injuries—whether self-inflicted or not—can be chemical, thermal, electrical, caused by radiation or light. As for the under-lying causes of a fire, they can be traced back to criminal mischief, destruction of property, revenge, crime conceal-ment, excitement, worship, and more. And we also have to consider the light under which we discuss and analyze them: criminal theories, philosophical debates, introspective thought. Yet we burn with intensity whether the fire was of our own making, accidental, or criminal. And thus, what are the necessary conditions for the ideal realization of the effort it takes to define the significance of flames? What do we take into account when defining the role fire plays in the world? Do we look at self-inflicted burns as wounds that tarnish its healing reputation or precisely the opposite? Regardless of whether we see its flames as purifying or caustic, the nature of fire is one of engulfing permanence. Whether it burns to destroy or to heal, fire—with its black smoke and blinding flames—passes with swiftness through our lives, sometimes abandoning us to complete darkness. The distinction between fire as cathartic element and fire as destroyer is not always as clear as it may be expected from two processes in antithesis, but if we look at the nature of the wound and the primordial role it plays in defining the concept of healing, the blurring of these demarcations acquires a more natural denotation. Over time I have found myself growing fonder of the idea that fire is like the serpent: their forms alike, both originators of primordial life. What a beautiful thought—the serpent, ectothermic, relying on the heat of its environment, is like the fire that warms our hands in the winter—a paradise of the mind one can never fall out of: to ponder on the nature of fire and the slithering of the serpent with the mind of an eternal child.   *pink! sunset~y*

Amaranthine flames hurried to decorate the sky as smoke and the smell of burned plastic and animal hair from rugs and winter blankets took over the south side of the village. It looked as if the fire was about to engulf everything in the courtyard and even spread to other houses, for there was no land between them. The fire threatened to consume all our homes, audaciously, like the shadow of death breathing upon the ones it will soon guide to another realm. This is how I imagined fire at that age, as death coming to claim what it was owed. As I watched the house burn, my mind rushed to how as children we would light bonfires in the street at night and play with blazing twigs, twirling them around in circles of fire that seemed to go on forever. No one was injured and with the help of the neighbors the family living there managed to save their livestock and poultry. But what was left of the house was not something one could call home any longer. My great-grandfather, who at the time spoke of himself as being a man as old as winter, lacked the strength to contribute to the building of the new house. When he was most lucid, he would spend his hours explaining to his daughter all that he taught her as a child, all the while scolding her for not choosing to follow in his footsteps. When the house was finished, his son-in-law took him to see it. A memory that has stayed with me as a beautiful and tender moment, although there are times when the sadness in his eyes comes back and pierces through me like falling icicles. I could tell he was troubled by the sight of a new house erected where his most loved creation once stood. I remember him being upset that they did not replace the plaque of the dead, an architectural element most houses in the village were adorned with. Made from granite or marble, the plaque of the dead had the names of family members who passed away carved on its surface—a house decoration memorializing the departed.

Years later, when I was in school, my class visited a Cucuteni-Trypillia site. It was there that I first heard of *the burned house horizon*. *Domiţhanasia*. Destruction of places by fire—destruction of homes by fire. In Neolithic Europe, the intentional burning of settlements for reasons that archaeologists and historians have still not agreed upon—in our small village, as we would later come to know, an act of forgetting about clothes left to dry on the stove. The idea of killing one's home, of destroying the place that is meant to keep you safe, warm, and nurtured, is something that has troubled me for a long time, and to which I return with both gentleness and anger. I found comfort in the thought of possessing such control: *to intentionally destroy a home*. Your home. But perhaps having no home meant I had no need to destroy it and I was merely fascinated by the concept of vitrifying the walls of an establishment until the colors born from the heat rehabilitate even the nature of the sky. My relationship with fire changed considerably throughout the years, the image I had of it became separated into various other images, depending on which perspective I was considering—whether it was that of teaching Andrei Tarkovsky's philosophy of film, studying the classical elements, or remembering personal experiences and celebrations. I sought the warmth of the fire even on torrid countryside nights, dancing around the flames in a white silk dress, a flower wreath on my head and red ribbons tied to my wrists. I sought its warmth when I encountered and tried to befriend the contrasting yet visceral reality of the city; its barbarism and architecture enveloping me for years to come.

Every eighty years or so, Cucuteni-Trypillia settlements were burned down completely, either before being abandoned, or at the end of each individual house's life. For houses had lives, and before building a new one, the old house needed to perish in amaranthine flames. With each of these acts of domithanasia, *the civilization of fire* wrote another page in the history that contributed to its rebirth. Since it was first described in 1889 at the tenth Anthropology Congress in Paris with the help of artifacts gathered from Fortress Hill (Cetățuia) in north-eastern Romania, the Cucuteni-Trypillia culture has fascinated archaeologists and the public alike. Although in modern times it is usually referenced in regards to the intentional burning down of its settlements, the aspect that I found most intriguing has to do with the small female statuettes that were found at the site. The twenty-one beautifully outlined figurines—the *Council of the Goddesses*, as they were later named—with their breasts and abdomens in different shapes and sizes—are now thought to have represented fertility kits that were offered to young couples after their formal union. Based on evidence from numerous shards and other findings, archaeologists believe that after the death of the woman, the figurines were shattered during a formal ceremony. The kits may have had the purpose of helping Cucuteni-Trypillia women understand their ovulation and identify their fertility window. The most beautiful statuette in the *Council of Goddesses* is also the one that plays the role of the primary figure, for it is the only one that is depicted with a hand above her mouth, in a pensive position. Last time I saw them, they were gathering dust in a museum deep in the heart of north-eastern Romania.

My great-grandfather passed away a few weeks after the new house was built, and thus his name was carved on a plaque of the dead, next to my great-grandmother's name and the names of the two children they lost in infancy. The people of the village came together one more time to build a house—a miniature of the one that was lost to the fire. The model house was placed on his grave after the funeral, on a Tuesday afternoon like all others. A small house that endured all that the passing of time threw its way for more than twenty years before it disappeared from the graveyard without anyone knowing what had happened to it. The notes my mind made of the day I went to visit his grave and saw that the house was gone have now taken on the shape of concepts I employ to simplify my idea of *becoming*—an organic transformation within time. The nature of time changes with each recollection I have of it: reversible or irreversible, progressive or ancestral, in linear passage or cyclical. The analytical breakdown of a concept that was once a memory that was once a moment in time that no one knows how it came to be. A headstone in the graveyard of all that *was not and will not be.*

Shrubs and saplings scratch my legs as I run deeper and deeper into the labyrinthine forest, touching its lower canopy with my fingers, projecting myself on the same background as narrative selves of exceptional destiny. What has left from my soul is revealed in error after error, it is grafted on my being in folkloric patterns of netherworld shadows and sleeping-poppies—an elegiac thirst for clashing with the senses of nature. The accident of living-dreaming-telling, along with its inclemency, gives birth to an impeccable archetypal space. No one is fighting me, yet I feel defeated. The faster my feet move, the more I sense I am losing contact with whatever world exists outside of this canopy entombed space protected by mythological creatures—I am becoming one with the trampling of wild boars, with deer and stags roaming freely, with maddening fairies, and spirits in flight. I am becoming one with the corpses of flowers and the fertile spasms of the earth. A desolate passion runs through my blood, temperamental features mark my face, poetic language emerges on my skin. A vital plenitude overwhelms me—a plenitude that must be kept in alcohol before using, just like the flaming words I put out inside my mouth. I stand naked in the heart of the forest, shedding in earthy textures not just a corset, not just skin, but my whole body. I walk around in a small circle, as if I have forgotten something. As if I have forgotten that death is already here—all trails take me to *her*, yet time is merciful, and I can still choose the longest path. I am standing before my-

self, an animal in human skin, a naked human borrowing the chromatics of the forest in order to become invisible. A ray of sunshine pierces through my core and impulsively reflects in the river. Trees from other dreams are in bloom. I wake up under the weight of dust on my arms.

I do not know how long I have been asleep, nor why such a specific memory appeared in my dream, albeit altered and consumed by the passing of time. When awake, I have very little recollection of it—just enough to know it is a memory and not a dream, like the poet who knows enough about his disease to say, "I am in agony, my wound is hurting—it has been trampled by the hooves of a thousand horses." I can hear the swooshing of trees outside, but I cannot move my body nor turn my head towards the window to see where I am. It does not matter—I am overindulging in the memory of a wound. I bear witness to myself and I am reminded of how, when I was little, I used to tie moon-flowers together with black ribbons in magical rituals meant to render me invisible. I fear chaos and pain. I long for devils to come, for they can turn water and sand into ropes, they can stop rivers from flowing into the sea. Using no threads or scissors, I braid flower stems in my hair. I release myself from the grip of words attacking each other inside my head, so I can tend to where the pain is coming from. With the delicacy of a hand that has yet to know impatience, I place rose petal after rose petal on the territory of the wound—not for healing, just to make it look pretty. I must still be dreaming, for I see the distorted faces of immortality—as fairy tale books have shown them to me—in each petal, whilst they become one with my injured skin. I feel the shape of ancient worlds under the silk ribbons around my wrists. Trees are in bloom, yet nothing can stop autumn from robbing our insides of all nostalgia and gently blowing it above our heads until the winter air freezes us like that: human, animal, emotion— together but disconnected. Hollowed out by rot and lured away by wild fingers, like the trees I was touching earlier, I make room inside myself for more dreams and certain disputable memories. I engrave my existence in a universe of signs and stimuli. Lying on a bed in a now completely dark room, the irregular verses of a fear-banishing spell I wrote as a child take wing above me with the emblematic ceremonial cadence of last days.

with hair of the wolf, I bind thee / I bind thee, nine-headed snake / I bind thee, root of eden rose / I bind thee, parched forest / I bind thee, river of dew / I bind thee, silver heaven / I bind thee, spirit of yearning / with hair of the wolf, I bind thee

Dreams and their ontic contours are unrestricted here. I used to believe that all dead people go to heaven, but not all of them are permitted to stay. As long as they are remembered by the living, they have a place within the grace of paradise. When I think of it now, I think how—like the rustling of a solitary leaf not yet touching the ground—a moment can trap within its lyrical self all the pains and wonders of the world. It takes but a second. A second for the world to become the perishable body of abscission. Why then has passing through life without leaving a mark always felt so enthralling? In another dream, I am living on a merry-go-round. An old coastline town, packed with tourists and water creatures in the summer. There are nights when it feels as if I am on life-support and leaving the merry-go-round would kill me. Saturday after Saturday, the laughter of children cuts through the morning air like train tracks through the alpine mist. Grain-girls sing their songs in a nearby field, which at night becomes what everyone refers to as *the valley of the fairies*. Spiders carrying healing water in their bellies live there with me—under the legs of porcelain horses, in between the lacing of tiaras, at the edges of carriages painted in the colors of hyacinths and water lilies. On the last evening of their vacation, the visitors carve maps of their hometowns in my flesh—a mythological geography rooted in the imaginary, often revealing their departure from the real. At other times, the children sketch leaves, flowers, and withering trees along my arms and legs.

And then, there are the words—in all languages of the world. *In caelo et in terra. L'ora del tempo. Cementerios llenas de huesos. Nemângâiere. Ideality. Anamnèse.* The merry-go-round never stops. It does not stop when the children no longer come. It does not stop when all maps and drawings and writings disappear from my body. It does not stop now, when the town is deserted. It does not stop when I wake up from dreaming it. In search of this dream, I change my appearance and move by the sea. In search of grain-girls and their communion with nature, I wear sand on my spell-casting lips and long for tainted certainties from the dreams of others. In search of hyaline descriptions and nothingness fashioned from flesh-like clay, I submerge myself in the representation of all myths.

I bind thee, nature / I bind thee, human / I bind thee, pen of the poet / I bind thee, language / I bind thee, clown mask / I bind thee, pillow / I bind thee, winter / I bind thee, angel / I bind thee, needle / I bind thee, melancholy / with hair of the wolf, I bind thee

I have always traveled with a hand on my shoulder. During blue ice walks in the middle of high Norwegian mountains, along trails crisscrossing foreign forests, in cities where fright transcribes itself on midnight windows—it also trembling—as the essence of souls brought together by aloneness. Towards the end, with nature in full genesis, closer and closer to the tragic dimensions I conjured with recklessness and euphoria. A hand that for years felt like a protective force guiding my path away from misfortune—only to later reveal itself as a memory of things to come.

I watch life unfold before my eyes, yet rarely my own. In dreams, in stories we tell one another, in books we read to each other at night. I watch evil spirits flying above ground, hungering for the hearts of the pure. I watch creatures of woods, waters, and underworlds perform their rituals on the walls of all my rooms—city after city, year after year. I watch life unfold, I witness rupture after rupture—time tearing itself apart under the fascination of fantasizing. I watch books turn to ashes—whispers becoming one with the wind. I touch hands that later disappear under blankets of snow. I feel the temporal restraints that have urged me into dreaming become the very air I breathe. My lips are still moving to the rhythm of the spell. I have been pulling words from this text even before writing it. Split from cosmic wholeness, mourning the viper bite we never knew. Dimensions, gestures, emotions. A thorn caught between the thigh and its flesh. A garden carved in bone within the space of a low tide. Blood roses frozen in the afternoon, like knees without a blanket.

In another dream, I dig with my fingernails in the soil of an unfamiliar garden. I write these dreams on sandstones and throw them into the sea—occasionally whispering words to myself, as if wanting to know whether there is something I did not remember. I dream of roving spirits from ancient myths making love to maidens at night. I dream of ghosts visiting me in my sleep, of fairies dancing in the air—I dream of skies opening up above my forest. In the winter, I dream of naiads taking me deep into the warm cavernous spaces of the earth, leaving pieces of my body in all waters along the way. I dream of monsters I drew as a child—of their grateful touch and petrifying voices. I dream that I am afraid of verdant nights and the screeching of owls.

I bind thee, hand / I bind thee, graveyard flower / I bind thee, music of our ancestors / I bind thee, page / I bind thee, pain / I bind thee, summer / I bind thee, word of unknown gods / I bind thee, ribbon / I bind thee, crossroad / with hair of the wolf, I bind thee

The spell never worked, and although I do not remember all its words, I hear the verses pouring down when it rains, as if I were casting it for my future self, under the auspice of fears to come. I do not think I would be traveling outside the realm of truth if I were to say that a lot of assertions about this and other similar times are just that—allegations of a polemic spirit. Bursts of emotional exhaustion. Diaries, journals, little notes we leave for each other—they are both mystifying and demystifying the truth of how we lived. Of how we are living. They build and demolish at the same time and with the same ardor—a continuous offering to an eternally famished audience. Admittedly, the fact that I refuse to draw connections does not mean they are not there, nor does it mean others will not be able to read the story. Yet the imaginary, the dreams, the voices, the fertile spasms of the earth, the blue ice walks, and the hand on my shoulder play a much vaster role in defining and lucidly revealing reality. "I am more beautiful than a pagan hymn." A line from what I think is an old poem. A poem that plays on the passage of time as a recurring theme—as do all other poems. Nonetheless, through the unforgiving specter of romanticism—which rarely makes us feel like there is a surface to dig our fingernails into in order to unravel hidden meanings—the passage of time loses its stroke. The mythical time of a poem about love becomes the whole of time. The undergrowth of the forest—landscape of fear, territory of wolves from the other side of the Danube. They say one must face all fears. I grew up being told that as a creature without any power whatsoever, I must not believe, just fear. A common conviction in all corners of the world, one that is best not to interfere with, the elders were saying. Yet I must face my fears, strip them of their skin and mask—I must face them in a never-ending replay of protection-seeking. I must run through the forest at night, descend into the well, take myself off life-support, rip the veins from my body when they no longer stay the course.

I still do not know how long I have been asleep, nor why I remember this particular thing and not others—it must have something to do with the *Days of the Wolves* celebrations. When I was about five years old, someone told me that my mother must have given me the name of the patron saint of wolves because I am a girl, therefore I will need all the protection I can get. Wolves, spirit guides from the world of yearning, creatures initiating the soul in the journey towards death, were highly celebrated in the village where I grew up. As children, we would gather around the fire to hear tales of summer wolves, of lone wolves and their unwillingness to interact, or of female wolves leaving their pack. In January and June, they were celebrated alongside their patron saints, much to the merriment of children. Yet, living so close to the forest and sometimes hearing their howling at night made me fear them. I do not know why I am remembering this, but I do know that the idea of skinning a wolf in order to face my fear was more terrifying than the fear itself. It must be why I wrote the spell with hair of the wolf—which was in fact used for other local remedies—instead of its skin.

I can no longer hear the swooshing of trees, although there are mirrors that show I am standing naked in the heart of the forest, with corpses of flowers in my hands. I think of the feebleness of not hearing myself breathe, of not seeing beyond what the mirrors are showing me. I think of how nature has rewarded my weakness with a ruthless gift: it has made me even weaker. When I stand covered before it, adorned with my best garments, wearing my voices as pearls on a string, I speak of the body as if it had never known the weight of the materials I am hiding it under. Its rehabilitation, the body's absolution from guilt—allowing invisibility to shelter me—is often what I associate with living in communion with the spirit, with nature, with everything reality has denied me. Yet how can I be invisible here, where the reign of natural hedonism speaks of corporeality with all its strength? Unable to walk around naked—like I do in my dreams—I see myself as an abstraction, as an invisible being hidden under layers of man-made flesh—I am excluded from nature. Injected with a sense of shame, with the urge to protect myself from what I do and what is done to me, I often turn to perceptual isolation in the middle of nature—a beautiful thing if you do not yet know what you are doing. Body and mind, blindfolded by their surroundings, softening the very landscape that is burdening me, in order to uncover a kinder reality than the one I was thrown into. *Abuse* becomes *incident*, *bruises* and *lacerations* become rose-covered *wounds, the skin of the wolf* becomes *the hair of the wolf*. My dead become the corpses of flowers. At the end of all poems intimate connections are revealed to us.

I bind thee, fear. With hair of the wolf, I bind thee.

III

A PAINLESS WOUND DOES NOT
CRAVE HEALING

The secret language of customs and superstitions surrounding funeral processions has always fascinated me. In some parts of Romania, coffins and tombs have rather intricate designs, and are often adorned with popular motifs such as flowers, trees, animals, or geometrical patterns. The symbol that most enthralled me was the one called the *thread of life* or the *path of life*. Drawing their inspiration from the representation of the labyrinth and the myth of eternal return, people carved three parallel lines on the margins of a coffin, lines joined at their ends by a diagonal weaving of intersecting paths so that our dead can eternally have a way of returning back to life. I have come across this symbol in many Eastern European and Mediterranean cultures, in various representations and with diverse meanings. Some of the elders said that the complexity of the design is in fact not meant to help the dead return to the world of the living, but keep them in the underworld. When she told me tales about the labyrinth, my grandmother spoke of the seen and unseen harmony of the world and how people can discover God when going through its trials aware of the three paths charted for us.

"Sin resides at the center of the world, and so does God," she used to say. For me, the labyrinth was this odd spiral I never knew how to draw.

Today is my birthday. I am old enough to tell myself I no longer desire any gifts. Yet as I was walking along the shore this morning, I came across twenty or so vertebrae in the sand and I decided to take them with me. I spent half a day interlocking the bones back together to form an incomplete spinal puzzle. A gift from the sea that I will forget here four months from now when I will return home. The hotel I am living in overlooks the Mediterranean and, for a couple of hours, the sun makes it seem like there are millions of tiny fairies dancing on its lustrous surface. Alas, the light hurts my eyes, so I pull the sheets over my head and let the murmur of waves guide my senses through the paraphernalia of memories I crave to bring to the surface. Shards of myth cleave my consciousness like swords through the body of the Minotaur. I quench my fragmentary and chaotic thirst for the beastly and the humane with the overly anatomized ruins of tales about to be born. As I penetrate the labyrinth, touching the wall with my fingers, its outside becomes the silk fabric entombing my body—I become the pulsating core of the labyrinth inasmuch as it becomes the fabric shrouding me in my journey towards the center. I descend into the darkness of my being, I retreat from the world into the cavernous depths of memories that have blended with my viscera. In the dark, my mind dwells on the creature residing within—the *monstrous I* and the shadows it projects. Just like no true labyrinth exists without its center, no descent into inner darkness is possible without confronting the creature that guards its core. My body moves and the swooshing of the sheets makes the whole process resemble that of writing—with eyes closed, I sink into my being and let my hands write on whatever surface they can find. Hidden deep within the rhythm of my gasps, the fragment breaks through the spaces I write myself in and out of. The fragment, often labeled a disease of language, always casting a mesmerizing gaze upon the mythology of the self. But today myth hides the meaning of what my core is telling me with the same fervor with which it breathes it upon the page. And thus, with eyes closed, I dig my fingernails into the contaminated soil of reality yet again. I dig my fingernails into the floor of the forest and the bed of the sea in search of carnal-scented roots to weave into my very own spool of thread.

The monotonous crunching of streetcars outside my window is heavy with the revelation of miracles engulfed in heat. It speaks of memory lapses and obsessive repetition of ontological motifs. Being and nonbeing, blending together so masterfully that death becomes the art of living and life a corpse outside of time. The absurd becomes the aesthetic norm governing a body existing and being erased simultaneously in the contradiction of the real and the illusory. A perfume bottle falls from the nightstand and my labyrinthine pursuit is already behind me. I've always believed that enclosed spaces and small containers make for perfectly sterile mediums in which to cut time without injuring the self. Hotel beds under white silk, armoires full of summer dresses and ribbons from the past, pockets full of sand, the alcoves of lost city gardens, perfume bottles. The oppressively humid air makes me think of cenotaphs and plundered graveyards. The deadness of the dead, the chaos to which we return time and time again, and how it becomes a space of subjectivity and individualized phenomenological degradation, a space in which we wander boundlessly through a constellation of tiny deaths unrolling the spool of thread that is supposed to help us journey back to the surface with repetitive gestures we no longer recognize as our own. When the mind collapses, bedlam enshrouds the body.

The weather is unpredictable here. I have never heard such a powerful wind nor have I ever needed its healing presence more than I do in this moment, a moment that will most likely get lost in my notebooks or washed off my arms by the sea tomorrow morning. The smell of frankincense follows me everywhere. An obsolete and insufficient reality that poses the problem of erasure under a different name. I sense it and certitude becomes a sin unto thought. For when you have thoughts, you know that asserting something with utmost certainty is a mere world of surfaces—the genealogy of transforming all that is bursting with matter into void and vice versa. And thus you pronounce yourself in favor of anonymous depths. I no longer care about following the path back from the center. Perhaps I never did, not to the extent to which I was told I have to. This too shall be freeing. I leaf incessantly through books bought from gift-shops and hotel lobbies, as if searching for something, although I have already read them and I know that their pages have nothing to offer. Nonetheless, I do not know how to stop my hands from frantically searching—they have outdistanced my mind a thousandfold. I think of past connections and whether the inner journeys of the people I once knew have ever truly intersected with my own. Have their trials brought them face-to-face with their Minotaur or are their labyrinths guarded by the same creature as my labyrinth? I do not remember enough mythology to know if such a thing was ever encountered, but the psychological and philosophical scraps of knowledge I hold tell me that it is not only a possible occurrence but a rather frequent one—to be inhabited by the demons of others. To salve the wounds of those you are not willing to abandon with diseased flesh taken off your quivering body. Perhaps even to shelter them within your carcass, providing thus not a remedy, but the delay of their demise.

Living in a time that feels fundamentally different from that of your peers is bound to bring about thoughts of creating one's own rituals in order to conjure a return to a sheltering center—the eternal return to the mythical age. And thus, the idea of slaying your inner monsters is no longer accompanied by the desire to exit victorious from the labyrinth. You crave its warmth and familiarity; you thrive in its nourishing womb. My rituals do not follow any certain patterns, nor are they the same each time I perform them; and perhaps if someone were to analyze them, they would not be rituals at all. I have always rejected all forms of repetition—for repetition means erasure. When I think about it, even the mundane actions and doings that one must perform on a daily basis do not follow any specific pattern. There is always something that I change, always something that I add or remove from the routine in order to shield myself from becoming repetitive. And yet, here are these rituals that help me travel to *the monstrous* and back, rituals that guide and protect me, or that at least provide me with the illusion of safety. Rituals like the one from this morning and all others. Today, when I am old enough to no longer desire any gifts, when I am old enough to know how to draw a proper labyrinth, I began my morning with a walk on the beach, as I have been doing every day for the past months. A walk on the beach heralded by black coffee on the street corner in a hurry and scribbling a few pages in my notebook before taking a shower. If I am to write in the morning, it is always before taking a shower, but never in a manner that makes it seem like something I have performed to the point of erasure. This morning, I wrote on the inside of my left arm. Three words, with my back against the sea and my eyes still closed. I wrote about no longer knowing how to get to the other. About how I perform rituals and walk paths that always lead me back to no one but myself. I wrote three words about how I reach out my hands to touch and all I feel is the coldness of my own skin. Three words about how there are mirrors everywhere and yet I am no longer able to see anything but fairies dancing for a couple of hours each day.

To plunge yourself into the depths of a labyrinth of your own making is to never escape it. To trick yourself that a prison of your own design is no prison at all. I wrap myself in silk and go back to writing about the forms and paths I still remember. A playful ray of sunshine falls upon the parts of my body I left exposed and asks to be allowed in but I turn my eyes towards the dark and let the sheets cradle me back to my center. Silk is the only fabric that touches the body in all the right places, the only fabric that both frees and entombs the flesh. When rendered into language, the rustling of silk stroked by throbbing fingers resembles the denotation of the labyrinth; into sound, it resonates with the battle cry of a thousand blades colliding with each other. Within an artwork, silk draws its strength from the calming glow of the skin it covers. Separating the soul from the body, the rustling of silk becomes a correspondence between the senses—it unfolds space and time, curving inwards, outwards, and back-and-forth upon the body as waves upon the shores of the world. In silk, the body falls for its captor.

***

Everything is wet from the morning dew. I sit on the terrace of a small café, tracing black lines on napkins as I wait for my breakfast. I draw in the same manner as when I was a child, without looking at the paper, without thinking of how my fingers hold the instrument with which I am creating something new. I draw almost with my eyes closed, capturing lines from within my mind and setting them free on paper. A few of them intertwine and the resulting figure bears a striking resemblance to a spontaneously rupturing wound, like the ones you see depicted in the pages of medical books. It resembles a rupturing wound because my pen has pierced the surface of the napkin, giving it the depth it needed in order to come to life. The word *dehiscence* comes to mind—the bursting open of a wound. When the edges of a wound are no longer able to meet. I crumble the napkin in my hand and pick another one from the stack to my left. I take a sip from the black coffee in front of me and more lines form themselves on the new napkin, as if my hand were being moved by a shape that is not yet there. Ink keeps on spilling into the creases of what I wish were a blank page, flowing like black veins through an imaginary ghost body. I could spend eternity here, waiting for my breakfast on the terrace of this café, next to deciduous trees, drawing wound-like shapes on gentle sheets of paper.

I have no memory of the first time I was wounded. I do not remember my first cut, my first bruise, nor the first time my skin healed. I remember falling, but I do not remember the very first fall. Threading a fine line between the earthly space and the mythological one, the first years of my life have protected me, not from injuries, but from the pain that usually accompanied them, since I was more fascinated with the folk nature of the healing process. I had no desire at the time to feel or know how long it takes for the body to repair itself, nor did I want to know how hemostatic time passes. The wounding of my body did not make me ponder upon impermanence. For when you reflect on time and its nature, regardless of the reason, you feel it running through your fingers—you want to trap it in the chains of your thought, to contour its shape and analyze its profile. Thus, my memories are limited to the countless ways in which my grandmother would salve a wound, to the homemade lotions and potions she used and the vivid bandages with which she covered my skin. As years pass, and you do begin to think about the nature of time, you find yourself enthralled by the image it creates as it slips through your fingers. Sometimes it appears as smoke hovering over a distant field, other times as a descent into chaos. The pendulum swings and wraps around your throat gradually, unwaveringly, tightening its grip the closer you come to understanding the inherent character of lost moments. Time past, lingering in memories, either tormenting or comforting us, either enlivening or erasing our traces. The mouth of the past speaks of time as the archetypal factor that births and kills all things. It speaks of a time that passes and never returns, creating a kind of life that can never be reborn in the same form as before. It speaks of a time that both shapes and devours us.

I have never responded particularly well to the idea that time heals all wounds. In the cruel light of chronic pain, time appears more as a menacing vortex than a gentle healer. Throttled by the careless forces of what pains us, of what drags us from latent conflict into open battles, healing takes on the role of an apparition passing through the hostile chaos. There are wounds that emerge never to be healed again—forever altering, deepening, enveloping all vigorous tissue. The softening and breaking down of my mind caused by prolonged exposure to environmental resistance of all shapes and forms has made me realize that, for the longest time, I trusted in the idea that as long as you know you are not well, that makes it alright. I sought guidance and comfort in nature, observing and analyzing in depth all its thorns, alterations, biases, and deformations. I have examined the way in which nature dealt and healed its wounds, regarding the abrasions of the body in the same manner as those of the earth in an effort to detach myself from everything I knew will never heal. Yet one does not need to be wounded in order to grasp that the desire to dominate healing arises from the desire to subjugate time. Unscathed, you can still crave the soothing thought that we might beat time by wisely predetermining our paths. Nevertheless, it is only through the present that we come in contact with the eternal. When you do not believe in the existence of an afterlife, dwelling obsessively on the thought of corporeal brokenness can become overwhelming. I cannot glance at paintings portraying the wounds of saints and find consolation in the thought that their suffering is detached from them, that it speaks more of holiness than it does of pain. And if I were to believe in an afterlife existence, how could I not believe that wounds mark us even there?

There is a line in *De Rerum Natura* that has traveled alongside my thoughts ever since I first read it—"and nature prompted man to shun a wound." The remedies that proved most effective have oftentimes come from the books I read and the trees I sheltered myself under. As with light filtering through the forest, I have withdrawn into their sepulchral, cheerful, or palliative pages with the confidence of the cornelian cherry blossoming in hostile environments. But reading too injures, it cuts through the mind—and sometimes even through the body—it carves its theories upon our own, it enfolds within our language the syntax of outsiders. As Baudelaire wrote in *Paris Spleen*, "we cut wherever we want—I my reverie, you the manuscript, the reader his reading"—words upon which I gazed with fondness when I decided to fragment and splinter my own writing. Reading becomes a blow, a shock that reverberates within us from the first book we touch to the last one we leave unfinished. Nevertheless, without reading, neither the wounding nor the healing we experience throughout our lives carry the same substance. The investigation of wounds and remedies that I undertook years ago in order to establish a possible confluence between the concept of the body in pain, the phantasmatic body, and the limitlessness of ways in which one can cut and scar the other has relied profoundly on words I read before ever knowing I would embark in such pursuit.

To say that the often misinterpreted momentousness of theoretical parameters might help clarify things is to say you have never experienced the intimacy, dirtiness, confusion, and delirium of a diseased body and all the tangled thoughts that come with it. There is no methodical comprehension of bearing the symbolic cuts of your ancestors, of gazing upon them and gradually transforming them into tangible wounds of your own. What becomes striking about the manner in which we overanalyze while simultaneously oversimplifying matters is the fact that, in doing so, we deny ourselves the process of healing through knowledge. Moreover, we deny the existence of healing altogether. For it is not in the gathering, analyzing, and simplifying of data that one finds answers pertaining to how the human surface displays its scars, nor to how the human interior repositions itself in alignment with a devastation that might or might not belong to us.

As the hours pass, the café becomes more crowded and the lines I am still drawing on napkins come together to form the shapes of snakes, recalling the time I would run barefoot through forests and poppy fields. The serpent, pressing its mythological and physical body against the grass, accommodating its narrowness within the folds of mind, paper, and the physical world of the past, swallowing its prey—letters, punctuation marks, words, ink stains; swallowing even the words left unwritten and the lines left unsketched. In his 1833 *The Worship of the Serpent*, John Bathurst Deane traces the origins of snake worship through folklore, tales of travelers, legends, and stories from antiquity—he follows the serpent in its slithering, from *the fall of man*, throughout his *redemption*, all the way to the decline of snake worship. In the preface, he describes his work as an attempt "to discover, in the mythology of every civilized nation, evidences of a recollection of the events in Paradise."

I am sitting in the crowded café, among strangers and cold furniture, pondering the act of injuring oneself and whether it originated from the first eye-opening event of our primordial parents. Having glimpsed the possible connections between our trauma and that of our ancestors— mythical or not—my mind dwells on whether the pain we inflict upon ourselves springs from our memories or those of others. On whether the blood gushing from the metaphorical wound does so in order to silence or arouse us.

In the eyes of the world, survival makes us hideous. We have become the cave-dwelling fish that lost their eyes to evolution, peripatetic through the darkness, with little oxygen and just enough food to sustain us until the next day. Adapting to our environment, having to shelter and rationalize our scarce resources; hungry for energy and light, avoiding predators, scavenging the dead for their remains, in compensation for our lack of sight. What is not needed, whether in the dark, in the light, or in life, disappears with the passing of time. Surviving through extraordinary measures exposes us to scrutiny, for the caves in which we retreat to heal threaten the serenity of a world savoring light—whether as reality or as the thing it aspires to reach, possess, and enslave. The city—a fairy tale bestiary, a serpentarium where reptiles are housed for exhibition. Witches, monsters, hags, wolves, ogres, ghouls—the minotaur, the glabrous man, the girl without hands, the flying vampire, the undead. Creatures that we once believed to have been walking the earth, returning in metaphorical form to better expose the wounds that scarred us.

According to folklore from Eastern European regions, those who are unfulfilled in the body—those who are marked, scarred, changed—also possess an unfulfilled soul. We do not fear them because of their appearance, we fear them because in the eyes of the world, an unfulfilled soul stops at nothing in order to achieve completeness. We fear them, for we know what we would do if we were to become them.

Mythology succeeds in an endeavor that both science and religion have not been able to accomplish: it brings together the body and soul and creates an entity that comes closer to portraying the reality of humankind. Whilst religion focuses only on the soul and science deals with the body—with matter—mythology and folklore acknowledge that we are not just our bodies, and we are not just our souls. Fairy tales take us by the hand and show us the way towards completeness, towards ourselves, and they do so by means of philosophy, rituals, mystery, elements of eternal return, subversion, metaphysical rooting, and beliefs in both monsters and deities. In *Romanian Bird and Beast Stories*, Moses Gaster describes fairy tales as elements "brought by the same movement that brought the tales and legends, customs and ceremonies—the new and the old, carried along by the same stream." The journey to the fantastic realm of the fairy tale is nothing more than our journey through time. A journey that does not rely on differences, it does not emphasize the qualities of the soul over those of the body and vice versa—instead, it thrusts us in both at the same time, offering us a shape to inhabit and abandon. The imagination of the human being walking hand-in-hand with the representation of sacred beliefs.

In Romanian mythology, the creatures one must fear the most are usually women who possess the ability to bewitch, enrapture, and hypnotize, who are able to fascinate and later devour those who stand in their way. Nymphs, wild fairies, witches, ragged old hags—keepers of wells and rivers, guardians of the forest, mothers or young girls who were wronged by their kinsfolk and took it upon themselves to seek revenge. Female characters who do not adhere to the customary ideals of beauty, meekness, submissiveness, or unworldliness that are often attributed to them. Romanian folklore holds these figures in close proximity not only to their compelling emotional and intelligent capabilities, but also to death and its representation in the life of a community. Our folklore portrays more than the fact that life contains death—it tells the stories of those who escape from its grip, the stories of survivors, of the men and women who stubbornly inhabit the castle long after the fairy tale has ended, depriving themselves of the splendor brought by reaching the end. Death is not a punishment, for destinies need to follow their natural course, and immortality is something not even a tale can offer—all rites of passage culminate in death. *Youth Without Age and Life Without Death*, one of the most treasured tales in Romanian folklore, does not have a happy ending, nor does it begin in a cheerful way, as fairy tales often do. Its first lines speak of a land enveloped by silence. Its battles are not between good and evil—its battles are fought for the right of humankind to live a life released from death's embrace. The conflict between truth and deceit in this tale that does not end in *and they lived happily ever after* is one that has been overanalyzed in the shadows by folklorists, historians, and philosophers alike. The story addresses the motif of the child who refuses to be born, which is a theme encountered in geographical regions from all over the world, yet buried somewhere in the footnotes and marginalia of folklore, for we cannot find ourselves in the heroes whose ending represents the return to the human condition they so ardently fought to overcome.

And yet, what I remember most fondly from folk tales and popular beliefs are not the rituals and superstitions relating to death and its importance in the community, but the references to the ultimate destiny of humanity. What I remember most fondly is the attachment with which folklore spoke of eschatological signs one should be aware of—signs that foretell the end of times. Waters overflowing, mountains collapsing, decapitated saints, winds sweeping up the ashes of the dead, darkened sun, bleeding moon, falling stars, poisoned rivers, warriors riding horses with lion heads and snake tails, comets, hail. Witnessing representations of the spectacle of time coming to an end, as prophesied through the ages, has provided me with a model for understanding how those around me often relate to being under the reign of a merciless time. For although the end was associated by most with ascending to the heavens, the manner in which that would happen was always devastating in nature. There was not a single being who believed one could go gently towards better realms—humans were foremost required to suffer the force of an apocalypse bestowed upon them by a divine paternal figure. In order to rise, one needed to become intimately bound with suffering—to break from their earthly bodies.

Returning to the concept of death and its primordial role in sequencing meaning and the manner in which humans should live and reach the end, I find myself wanting to emphasize the ghastly presence death has in dreams. In the necessity of knowing what will happen to them, what will wound and heal them, what will lead them into perdition and what will bring about their ascent towards the celestial afterworld, humans have created a most enthralling framing of omens. Eastern European folklore depicts a fascinating representation of the death omens that come to us in dreams—sometimes going as far as to describe in great detail the manner in which that end will occur. If you dream that you are walking through a graveyard at night, it means you will die alone. Dreams of animals, birds, and insects—horses, blackbirds, or bees—represent a collective death. Yet if one were to thoroughly dig through these nocturnal premonitions, they would find that most of what we dream at night was chronicled at one point as an omen of death. Drowning in muddy waters, drinking alone on a hill at night, snakes in the garden, picking mushrooms after the rain, seeing your face in a mirror at the funeral of a loved one, brushing the hair of a doll without eyes, falling from the highest branch of a tree, windowless rooms, insects crawling under your skin, stealing something from a corpse, veils, broken mirrors, doors in the middle of no-where—all omens of impending death, the ultimate rite of passage.

And thus, in the eyes of the world, survival makes us hideous. Picking a fight with death and emerging victori-ous nevertheless scars and shapes us into fay creatures—it tells the world that we have strayed off course, that the mis-matched body shelters a maddened soul, for no protagonist can take on death and return to wander the earth in sane-ness. In an encyclopedia of beasts and monsters, the story of the man who sought life without death would go on for pages, for life without death is a miscreation, a perversion of our passing through time, and nothing makes us more monstrous than refusing to accept who we are.

"I must think of this place as a nineteenth century West Bohemian spa," I say to myself. As soon as I let the words travel through me, my mind finds refuge in the memories of others, in the romanticized version we now have of forest-embraced European sanatoriums, with their peculiar diets and thermal treatments. Until his death in 1823, Goethe visited the spa town of Karlovy Vary more than thirteen times, where he used to take lingering walks alongside Beethoven, much to the delight of the locals. Mark Twain often spoke of wallowing in the mud of Marienbad. Chekhov died some miles away from Baden-Baden after a sip of champagne, a camphor injection, and a few weeks of strenuous writing. According to the newspapers of the time, his body was brought home in a refrigerator car used for transporting oysters.

Waking up for breakfast every morning at six is the only constant a place like this can provide me with. I sit next to a window hidden behind thick curtains covered in dust and the ghostly silhouettes of everyone here. I find myself comfortably embraced by the nightmare of the night before. A cup of black tea and a tangerine placed in front of me play their part in keeping the romance alive, reminding me of Chekhov's strawberry tea. The first thing they tell you here is that you need to stop writing. I break open the tangerine with my hands and discover a world of memories embedded upon its skin. I see the colors of a Maltese sunset, the many rivers I've left behind, and then a reflection of the person crying two tables away from me. I see the whole of Florence in this already decaying fruit. The theater of the world, courtesy of time passing painfully slow. I see the portrait of Simonetta Vespucci, naked, with a snake twined to her necklace. A sip of black tea makes my tongue taste lines from *De Hominis Excellentia* about physical pleasure as the antithesis of human dignity. I close my eyes craving for the quiet touch of a god that never was, needing to know why there is nothing inside—needing to know where does the divine soul that accompanies a decomposing body reside.

I first heard the term *confabulation* when I was studying philosophy of mind. Although I prefer *memory error*—a misinterpreted memory of myself or the world I am living in. A fabrication that carries me in its arms through passages and glorified ideas of sanatoriums, camphor, and rivers flowing downstream. Adrift, under the weight of an audience, I feel incarnated into the flesh of all others. Relying on the reversibility of moments, I oversimplify my responses to the movements of time, I choose other paths, I write of other possibilities—an addendum to the current reality that makes me realize I can never coincide with myself. Yet the world remains the same. I am guilty of not being there. I think of pouring my words into the veins of the Seine. I clutch mentally at every object that meets my eyes. I speak in Dostoevsky's words about my fondness of striving for ambiguity. There are no limits to breathing in this chaos. I see historical female figures merging with thoughts on primordial *oneness* and attempts to affirm myself without mirrors embedded in the skin of a putrefying tangerine.

The little that I remember is not enough to build a biography. Regardless, I am halfway there. My fingers are now tracing scars on a body that does not belong to me. The *philosophical body*—breathing in the subtle yet piercing sound of my thoughts clashing once more with waves, trees, other bodies; with paths running through narratives of worlds ending and silence overlapping sanity like threads slithering upon the paths of the labyrinth. A stranger explains to me how fortunate I am that these scars are hidden under clothing and ink. She does not know of the new scars, the scars that are not there yet—mere wound awaiting healing. Plain. Ordinary. Cruel. An anti-metaphysical perspective on decline. I studied her voice as one studies the functions of organs in the body. A metaphor for ends to come. An ironic correspondence between two hospital beds. A poem.

Night after night, the same dream: glass coffins, dirt, and worms crawling on my feet. I wake up and write about excess, collisions, plagues, tighter ropes, indifference, forests. I convey absence through violet veins, weary eyelids, the sound of skirts ruffling outside the window. I write, although I am not allowed. I write to know I am not dead. An insect still in flight. The sound the rope makes when wrapped around the thigh. There is an entire world outside the gates of this place, but all I see behind the curtains is the mirroring of my monstrous insides. I return to gathering things in my hands. I gather words like the sea gathers all flesh under its heaving embrace. I am devoid of semantic connections, in service of rapture, progressively infusing my blood with the refusal of immortality. Everything binds and unbinds the future in the form of riddles crisscrossing on my flesh. In dreams, in sickness, in darkness—inside me.

When I was a little girl, I used to tell everyone that I wanted to become a doctor and heal the world that Eve had quarantined with her sin—with my sin. Penitence, running through the veins of a child who was taught that women hold the world hostage with the deceitful control of their minds. Rejecting that life, I took on the role of a curator. I took on the biblical persona, promising myself I would free her of guilt, of blame, of the world having to end. One by one, I gave myself all names: Antigone, Ariadne, Nausicaa, Miriam, Lilith, Eve. I took on the graves of those before me—of the nameless, of the named, of the loved and the unloved. I took on the graves of those who followed. I devoted time, hands, and silk ribbons to killing my own narrative so that everyone else could keep theirs. Searching for the possibility of uprooting, saving the world from having no telos other than self-perpetuation.

To walk these streets is to affirm life. To walk these streets with a throbbing pain is to affirm that no anguish is more formidable than the image of my footsteps leading me nowhere. I pass by the Maltese national library in search of a pharmacy. I ask for a painkiller and the woman behind the counter hands me something called *Moment*. In Valletta, where time always feels unreal, where mirrors are not needed because I have the sea, the glowing of my skin, and the silver on my fingers, I look down at my hands and forget where I am going. Stepping outside the pharmacy with twelve *moments* in my hand, I check the weather forecast to see how many of them I will be needing. The city brings to light marble blocks taken from Proserpina's temple in order to embellish its other buildings. I think of rain, of Petrarch, of a Stratford map I keep as bookmark. I think of cognition and aspects of the human mind that I will never fully grasp. I pause to read a paper on instinct blindness and it almost convinces me that this is something I must overcome at all cost. That I need to escape the confines of the I—*the adult I, the primitive I* of my childhood, *the monstrous I* of my nights—to escape my own voice, for what we see is what we are not, never what we are. Pages later, I read that intuition is a rich guide yet it suffers from something I no longer remember, therefore, in my mind, it just suffers. I think of needing theoretical guidance more than ever.

Walking the streets of Valletta, I refine versions of the same thought in a voice that only I can hear. I tell myself stories about Thomas Mann's unfinished writings, about flying blind—stories about maps drawn by German cartographers. Memories heal me, therefore I am always in need of more memories. More waves. More bodies. More flesh. More painless wounds. More ashes. More connections. More reckless abandon. More masks surging from the void. I am always in need of more gramophone needles to scratch the surface of the dying tomorrow. I feel myself becoming a temporary restoration to the world above, much like Proserpina's blocks of marble. In my mind, I touch the softest fabrics, I engage in conversations about pleasure-loving ethics, I sketch the beginning of the nineteenth century.

I take another sip of black tea and the beauty of being an animal with remarkable intelligence lost in literary techniques and psychological concepts comes to mind at the same time as Boccaccio's thoughts on accepting all pleasures. The thought comes to me not in words, not in sounds—it comes as a skin-deep crusade. The crusade of an animal wounded by humans, unable to crawl back into the forest. I turn towards the person sitting two tables away, wanting to have a voice so I can tell her stories of walking the streets of Karlovy Vary one summer afternoon; stories of champagne, camphor, and wallowing in mud. I study her face in search of other women, other monuments, other names. I want to speak, but the entire world thunders against me. I am invaded by memories of when the water was calm. Nevertheless, it is not enough to build a biography.

Exhausted fingers trace the curves of a book like amorous grasshoppers descending from white opium poppies. Thunder gnaws at time while raindrops dig tombs for the memories of our memories. Bedridden thoughts fill one notebook after another. There is a lighthouse in my dreams—a lighthouse in which pillows of flesh adorn the bed with oneiric creases of souls bathing in Lethe. When I awake I think of Baudelaire's funeral marches, of his soul as a tomb, of his transmuted metamorphoses, then once again allow my head to fall upon the violet pillow. If *the soul of the poet is a tomb*, then poems are nothing but compositions of fleshless cadavers, plants, insects, and the ever-blazing fires of rottenness—spiders, serpents, and roses amidst stanzas and memories of walking barefoot on the putrefying floor of the forest. Heat and hunger engulf the night as corpses emerge from the silent voice of pouring rain. I think of the many names I gave to the manner in which my hands tremble when I can no longer remember that there are mirrors everywhere. Nonetheless, memories of time, space, decay, the void, and the annihilation of desire come to me in the form of an abhorrent struggle to seek redemption. When describing fetish aesthetics based on the urgency of not succumbing to futility, one can't help but turn to Baudelairean temporality. Time, not as the collapse of everything into the eternity of space, but as a two-headed snake—the past and the future. The smell of frankincense follows my every move, lingering on every page I touch. I get lost trying to retrace a map in the air.

Memories creep up under the covers and in the cracks of the shelter I have built for myself with preposterous rapidity. Memories of Monet receiving Japanese lilies right before he died. Memories of streams in pure contemplation. Memories of all that is human. The same music echoes every morning—music that hides the freedom to roam between its notes. Free as an insect breaking the walls to the past—an insect that becomes more and more insane with each breach. In hunger for harmony rather than in conflict with its demands, each consciousness seeks self-recognition through the metaphorical death of *the other* and by aspiring to kill or negate the ones it seeks in admiration, the ones in whom it mirrors itself. To kill or negate hidden faces radiant with longing, hands trembling with primitive touch. *The self*, reduced to the fear of losing itself in *the other*.

A veil falls over the abyss. The here-and-now takes on the shape of an illusion. The decay of the flesh resembles the imprisonment of the poet. The moment is already gone. There is no life without death. There is no meaning without loss. Despite the suffering, despite the conflict, despite the coherence that can only exist in a life legitimized by the existence of death, each consciousness seeks self-recognition. Self-recognition through the attraction to speak, through the precipitated attacks of the gaze, through passion and sublime drive—through the cruelty of courage, through the game of loving and allowing yourself to be loved. Self-recognition in travelers, prisoners of the road, whose souls were lured by the silence of this or any other voyage only to end up tasting too little from the bitter, the old, the new, the gradual, and the forever. Tasting too little from dust mingled with ashes and sea salt, with identity, with their *self* from years ago and their *self* from years to come. Were it not for the constant threat of erasure, fragments of my persona would continuously struggle to escape the scrutiny of self-reflection.

I always had a soothing connection with the poetry of Anna de Noailles. In *Stars that Behold the World*, a poem written in 1915, she speaks of our dead watching over us from the height of the heavens and the world entrusting its redemption to the sacredness of death: "you die! / conceive that it is too heavy a weight / for those who in their grave and burning sadness / have always confused life with love." I now associate her words with feeling safeguarded by the unknown. Were it not for the collapse brought by death, a part of me would eternally be unable to reach *the other*. Still, I make no attempts to hold on to static images. I do not gaze upon the remains. Ash among ashes. The return to the world of the living. Nothing but words and half-realities relying on the force of a wild train station draught to be carried farther and farther. Fractured truth puts me closer to the void, and at the same time, closer to the fantasy of fulfillment. Discontinued thinking becomes a way of life, a way of embracing said void, while negating its existence. I strive to create my own private language of screams and gestures and sighs.

After Eugène Boudin invited him to paint on the beach, Monet decided to become a painter. He painted instead of working. He decorated his house with bridges, painting them time and time again. Self-reflection takes me to places I do not wish to visit. It takes me within the human mind, in the afterword of a book, in the warmth of an embrace I thought forgotten. Self-reflection takes me in a phrase that mimics Monet's brush vocabulary. It makes me feel that tomorrow is already here. All such endeavors affect the body in a manner that, if you were to put in words, it would once again lead you to Baudelaire—to his decomposition within the realm of nature. If you were to paint it, it would resemble gentle summer days, the simple days that one gazes upon in museums, the days of weakness and peace and darkness whispering from old paintings of a time so frail and yet so perfect. But my days are senseless, and consciousness has become agonizing. The need for reason carries nothing but decay, despair, absurdity, and isolation. Everything is permitted yet nothing is possible.

Much like impetuous rivers that cannot be mastered, music is both overwhelming and cathartic. It gives me the strength I need in order to keep feeding on *differences* and also to assert the *different*. I feed on modifications, alterations, and changes; I become the cluster of plants in the pond that might poison the animals drinking from it. There is no need to place your hand on a wound to feel it throbbing in pain. There is no need to see its root to know that a tree is dying. I am renouncing history. A film frame has lost its meaning. Vain and cruel, I have become a *self* that contains all negations to come, I have escaped the universe of time and space—page after page, touch after touch, train after train. I have become the idea of a sea beast moving in the deep. I have become the labyrinth. I am entombed in poetry. In the first stanza, in the last, in the blueness of thirsting ink—in the bruising of eternity. I have become alone. I am alone.

Reveling in both illusion and splendor, turning wakefulness inside out, I offer myself a Barthes-inspired moment, a realignment of the senses, an instant in which the eye becomes the prime organ of perception. By acquiring the atmosphere of the rain and aesthetically fetishizing my surroundings, I have at last become an allegory. I have become an allegory for the sake of evading the trappings of a common existence. I have awoken to the sound of inner noise, detached from life—secluded in a place I could never call *home*. Yet I hunger for even more distance. Distance from the place I can only revisit in my mind, as the memory of an untouchable time, the place I carry within me everywhere I go. I have curated myself into an escape artist of spatial closure, with nothing to do but wash the seconds dripping down my flesh so that there are no eternities beyond the time it takes my gasping mouth to consume the air that conceals the capacity to change or move me. I choose the aesthetic over the ontological.

Sometimes catching my reflection in a mirror is all it takes to find myself outside, sitting on a fence in someone else's memory of home. A film: a white, white day. Opening credits roll on a black screen. Music, and a place in time becomes a place in mind. Exile becomes the newsreel. As the camera moves, I am running through the rain, becoming the embodiment of impatient synapses and brightness caused by self-imposed amnesia, cutting time in its most famished moments, feeding the memories of others to the gaps I leave behind in my own. A small bird lands on someone's head. Tarkovsky is one of the few who knew how to portray the role played by memory in matters of exile, when your inner world gains the ability to mimic the shape of all other worlds—a gathering of memories synonymous with fulfillment, as one can no longer go back to a physical home, but to a place in the mind. You become the artist, relentlessly pursuing your muse beyond all frames and pages, beyond the fragility of your body and the bodies of others. As I wash my hair mimicking the gestures of a person who does not exist, plaster falls from the ceiling and home becomes nothing but a movement in a dream—a dream in which you can never enter the house. You become a fire in the field. In exile, nothing is invented. The episodes of grief can be anyone's. The pain of others pierces through you. Voiceover and timeframes connect your memories to those of film characters who speak of home. Erasure becomes a second skin, a nocturnal tale that you cover yourself with during the day. In exile, mundane beauty is forbidden. Every poem has to be the greatest of poems. Every confession has to be bursting with meaning. In exile, flesh and bone no longer stay together. In exile, excess governs the gathering of memories that serve as shelter. I have a vision of my mind sharing discourse with *another*, not in language as I know it, but in gestures made of flesh, bleeding paper mouths, and the noises of time. A vision of bodies decaying as flawlessly as black-and-white images, so sharp their edges could cut my eyes just by looking at them. I write it on my skin as marginalia in a manuscript to later make room for it amongst my other memories. I do not exist here. Like a Bach fugue in the Black Forest, displacement becomes the territory of a dream I traverse half-consciously. And if ecstatic blissfulness represents the sole possibility of tending to the ontological rupture between consciousness and life, between the individual and the world, then achieving it can only happen when I have embraced the agony caused by that rupture, for a painless wound does not crave healing.

Sinking into warm water turns my body into a map. Blue veins, freckles, curves, scars, inked words—charting the places I will no longer call home, trailing the path I will no longer walk on, speaking in languages I may never learn, revealing from under my skin coordinates of hands I will never touch. Under warm water, my body becomes a terrain of possibilities long departed, the remainder of the cluster in which I was born. Possibilities never existing, possibilities not yet discovered. If perception is merely the effect of a discreet stimulus, then visibility comes with this funereal submerging of one's flesh into native water. At home—morning, midnight, at all times. For the sake of a simplicity I still crave, I have Bach keeping me company. Sound becomes a cavernous afterthought consuming my being at the intersection of sexual urge and philosophical reflection. My fingers are exposés from old books, a Proustian shock to the senses, auxiliary lines tenderly mapped for no one and all to find. My very own arterial mapping—the tributaries of a river at dusk.

In Romanian, *înrâurit* means influenced by something or someone. It comes from *râu*, which means river—to be *inrivered*. I never dug deeper into the etymological origins of how the word was formed, for its meaning was always quite clear to me, as I knew from early age that all waters carry a prevailing influence on people—I knew by heart all superstitions and popular beliefs pertaining to water. You must never quench your thirst from a well, river, or fountain at night—especially not in the forest. For through that water, beasts, fairies, naiads, nymphs, and other mythological creatures—as well as the souls of the undead—will enter your body and never abandon it. This painted a marvelous picture in my mind. Whenever he was asked about his use of rain, Andrei Tarkovsky would say that nothing is more beautiful than water. And nothing was more beautiful to me than water carrying fairy-tale creatures and souls in need of a home. In fact, until the village priest scared it out of me with threats of spending eternity in damnation as a body inhabited by the soul of another, I made a habit of drinking from all waters at night. Situating magic on the same plane as religion was a common occurrence, therefore replacing one belief with another, although it was something I heavily protested, felt somewhat natural. However, depriving oneself of the magical perspective of superstitions and popular beliefs was not something one did in the village, which is why everyone found their own manner of piecing together the two—sometimes even by favoring magic. For when it comes to the unknown, replacing it with the power of magical thinking not only helps propagate those beliefs, but it also makes it easier for people to dwell inside them without fear, which is why analogies are rarely needed—in fact, superstitions and popular beliefs abound in disanalogical arguments.

I have what people call shy veins. Difficult, slender, stubborn veins—a body, highly textured, yet refusing to expose its blueness. Sinking into warm water changes that. Pursuing their own need, my veins flow like rivers. They flow down the crease of my spine, they flow along my arms, they flow on my left thigh. My veins flow and leave behind a map of all the Russian and German words I never learned. They flow around my ankles, tracing the wrinkles of sheets I never slept in. Individual streams of blood— forced, disciplined—coming together for the creation of a beautiful thing that can only survive under warm water. Reminiscent of Caravaggio's red folds of fabric, my blood plays on the need of its surroundings—the bodily depths need the materiality of the surface and the perspectives of space in order to envelop darkness and light.

I am always writing something inside my head. If I were to write a poem, it would be a poem about the absence of a universal meaning. A meaning that we none-theless simulate at night, during slow and strenuous walks along the narrow alleys of botanical gardens of violets or poppies or lilies. It would be a poem about every new thing that I read, every new thing that fills me with snarling grief and throbbing thoughts. I would write a poem about all that leaves me thrusting for warmth and calm. It would be a poem about how I put my clothes on with the image of an-other me in my mind, watching blood dripping on the floor of a waiting room—a poem about the demands of conver-sation and people growing so tired of it that they have now replaced it with journals and diaries and notes abandoned on solitary nightstands. If I were to write a poem, it would be a poem about the overwhelming abstraction of going back to writing without knowing where it will take me next. In warm water, I ask myself what is to become of my dreams when reality emerges so wounded that it no longer stands for anything other than fantasy and make-believe. I ask myself what will happen when I become an irrational character of tedious mornings, pulling myself up from sapid slumber with no other purpose than to reveal my body to the light of day. If I were to write a poem, it would be about the lines I memorized along the way, the threads I used to sow wounds, the knives I used to carve open paths—the words I used to feed my mouth when it was starving in the dark. It would be a poem about the moment when the air will suddenly disappear, making us plead with suffocation for new bodies, for new forms to inhabit in an airless world.

Metaphorically casting my skin in an effort to achieve real deathlessness, I remember that underneath a painting of Jeanne Duval, Baudelaire wrote *quaerens quem devoret*—searching for the one she will devour. I think of how, in rocking chairs, thirty years from now, we will remember not his *Black Venus*, but reading once, in a book about myths of nature, the story of the first hummingbird and the frolic of flames that did not heed our words. When the water was calm, when the wound was still amaranthine red—as red as the horizon painted by burning houses— when savage rites wrote themselves from memory onto the pages of black notebooks, I abandoned myself to the idea of real deathlessness. In the calmness of warm water, deprived of the familiarity of living, my being becomes aggressive towards itself. The ridiculousness of being alive, not as a creature of flesh and bones and blood and movement, not as object—not even as void (a void)—but as chains and cages and bars. Forced to weave the thread of time hoping for a safety net; getting yet another proof of uncertainty. If I were to write a poem, it would be about the knowledge of not being able to find a flower resembling touch. A poem about accepting life without beliefs and universal meanings—being alive as a concept that no longer applies to any of us.

As I silently lower my head in the water, as my gasping mouth struggles to break the patterns of freedom, my veins flow yet again and turn my thoughts towards reality. It is necessary to have blood in your veins. It is necessary to know what inarticulate convulsions are. How to scream, how to weep, how to gather yourself. How to listen. It is necessary to embrace corporeal excess, sensory chaos, and the breaching of the flame, just as a forest embraces the disengagement of its canopy. To experience something both as object and mere façade. To be both the space and the monster that has invaded it. *Being-ecstatically-beside-oneself*, a baroque ceiling engulfing consciousness-conditioned language. Consuming the voice—the pure voice acting as agent of other languages. Death, desire, and discourse become space. Sexual and spiritual urges balance the flow between the fatal and the harmless. The one color that remains constant is blue. It is necessary to have blood in your veins. A body can connect with another body; a world can connect with another world—a voice can collapse into another voice. We can live with ourselves. Through metaphor, the poet rewrites the world. Through the gentle madness of warm water, blue veins remap the affinities between flesh and possibility. By deliberately extending the time I spend in water, I am not just burdening my memory with multiple sensations, I am also keeping the process alive, recreating memories that have abandoned me. Much as the movement of film cameras struggling to capture the sea, moving my limbs and torso is crucial to the manner in which the blueness decides to expose itself. The movement of my right arm erases a city as it emerges from the water.

I once lived in a place where it took thirty-nine flights of stairs just to shut the door. A place free of mappings, sightseeing, tumults, blood, veins, heart as an open wound—free of intimacy and flesh. Today, my veins flow like rivers. They flow, and September comes. They flow, and my arm no longer shuts that door. Day after day, I open the window, I sink into warm water, I watch maps being created—whether in dreams or in abandonment. I envision annihilation through the eyes of children, lightness through the eyes of mothers. I envision the afterworld mirroring the paths of the forest at midnight. I envision

Prague merchants, languages projected on the ocean floor, a poet's bonfire, Margarita Terekhova in a film frame on the other side of loneliness. Stratum upon stratum of flesh and language as I extend to more than just my body, as I collect materials for the script, for the poem, for the stories—for conversations with another.

The world is falling apart, and yet to sink is to keep the possibility alive. I long to place a comb in my hair and wear skirts that fall to the knees in pleats. I long to read a book on poisons. To run away. To send you flowers. I long to visit a morgue. To be the most beautiful character in my journals. Naked against the dark eternity, as the world falls apart—mapped, adorned, liberated. I long for the waltz of silver birches, the soul of a landscape, the cynicism of a fading print, the shadow of a starving train. To believe in metaphysics and to be born in all sorts of mortal shapes. I long to prevent death, war, killings. The list becomes as suffocating as my childhood dreams of skies opening up above me. I taught myself to write with my head under water—I taught my fingers to become both the word and the medium. Language is indeed a skin, and the whisper existed before the lips. My veins flow like rivers and a word appears next to the birthmark I forgot I had. It appears like a grove of trees in a Tarkovsky frame—voiceless philosophical aporia. It appears as a starling outside my window.

IV

DEATH ASSEMBLAGE

Existence is always corporeal—we bleed, we ache, we become wounds. Our lovers must embrace us in this form and sully their flesh with ours. The physical manifestations of our becomings and experiences leave traces on the world and on ourselves—the body marks the mind. We hold each other, and the mind marks the body. Regardless, the process feels lighter than all non-physical embraces, for in all that is physical we put aside our pain and forgive—we offer our corporeal existence, therefore exposing ourselves incessantly to the touch of others and to that of time. And time passes in an odd manner when we wait for things that are out of our control, as if the hourglass had shattered yet the sand is still pouring, only there is infinitely more sand, and it is pouring inside you—drowning your bones in inept seconds as it devours your flesh. The idea of death becomes a wound that we inflict upon ourselves in order to heal, in order to pass through life—feeling, loving, gathering. The act of *perishing* reminds us of our own impermanence. We gather within ourselves the fossils that will later be discovered and embedded at the site of our demise. And thus, time matters to us more than death. As humans with free will and the ability to sometimes influence the course of our lives to our liking, we think that we can discipline its passing and the marks it leaves upon us, more so in response to traumatic events.

Tachypsychia defines the neurological condition which alters our perception of time either by lengthening it, slowing it down, or contracting it. A blurred vision, time as a collection of unrelated passages, fossils traveling to the place where they will be discovered by the living. Time as inked reflection, as paradise lost, as untruth from beyond the bones. Time as blackbirds outside my window. Well-captured intentions—the same throughout all journeys, a prose poem, aberrant brushstrokes that touch my face, stitched together with no apparent plot, no connection to each other aside from a rite of passage and the space in between. A neurological condition in which we alter time to give ourselves the possibility of passing in goodwill through the home of the dying.

It happens everywhere. It happened on the stairs of Montmartre, it happened on the bridges of Budapest, in the death mask museum, along the white stone wall of a country library. It happened in the house with ten rooms connected by nine doors. Nine doors of different colors, leading to their very own unique universes—all gathering memories, gestures, fossils. The green door opened the room to dolls I could only play with on special occasions and the death paraphernalia my grandparents had collected throughout the years. When you would open the red door, the scent of homemade gingerbread would take your mind away from all exterior influences and mishaps. The blue door led to my room—a room with two small beds, one desk, and a big armoire in which I kept the silk ribbons I used to trap my hair in the mornings.

It happens in the house at the edge of the forest. It happens on the coastline of a secluded yet crowded island. It happens inside the castles we visit along the way. It happened after I found out why birds wait outside the home of the dying. The passage of time—altered by neurological conditions or not, from thought to paper, from wounds to scars, from skin to fossil—happens everywhere.

Nothing is as beautiful as the mental space that has no obligation to bear meaning or name, no obligation to revolt against its primary form. Born in my mouth and blindfolded by the hands of another, a mental space not demanding change—immediate, infinite, uncertain—a narrative feeding on contact, on the healing and reopening of wounds. The whole of time and space, imprinted on a singular moment, on the moment of going slowly down the stairs with arms full of books and flesh made of poems. Nothing is more beautiful than the mental space on the outside of an inside quivering in theories of love, life, death, the afterworld. I hold a mirror close to my mouth, corrupted yet revealing of breath, love, and the idea of being smeared all over the room. It happens everywhere. I am posthumous, yet so alive. In passports, in gestures, in words that are never hollow. Posthumous, yet bound to keep on speaking of mental spaces, diagnoses, shapes, and answers. Nothing is more beautiful than the mental space disguising itself as paintings, manuscripts, and sculptures from ancient times; speaking of symbiosis between the life of mortals and the life of mythical creatures, angels, idols, monsters. The passage of time, altered not by a neurological condition, but by the bruises left behind by delusions of mind clashing into each other when I need it the most—a worthy replacement of the voice I once heard.

It happens at home. I am home. Most of my things are scattered all over Europe. There are rats in the streets. Tourists come here searching for mysticism, for the sacred and the profane, for fairy tales and healing wellsprings. They come to trail beautiful mountain paths, lose their minds in seaside clubs—they come to visit the home of Dracula. There are rats in the streets and time passes as it always does. I am standing outside my parents' apartment. My keys do not work. I turn my head to the left and see a door that looks familiar. A two-bedroom apartment, home of Silvia and Boris. They moved to Bucharest from Northern Romania as young students. He became a writer; she became a museum curator. I am ten years old, coming back from school, hurrying to spend with them the hours until my parents come home from work. Their apartment is small—there are books and statues everywhere. It always smells like coffee and Bulgarian rose perfume. She is as beautiful as in her youth, and when I grab her hand, the first thing that comforts me is that it is as cold as mine. She rocks me to sleep with Bach, a tradition that I sacredly kept throughout my life—falling asleep to Bach, calming my nerves to Bach, sinking into warm water to Bach. They never had children of their own. When Boris died, Silvia went mad. She would drink coffee liqueur in the mornings, then wander the streets with photos of him pinned to her bathrobe. My parents told me not to visit her anymore. All the children in the building were told to stay away from her—she'd gone mad; therefore, she was dangerous. The cold hand that rocked me to sleep, fed me, read me ethnographic research papers and taught me the word *thanatocoenosis* now belonged to a mad woman. Nobody talks anymore of her as the beautiful and kind museum curator who became a writer in her old age. Nobody sees her as the caretaker of neighborhood children. She is now the madwoman filling our heads with ideas on the death of god, the beauty of meaningless rocks she and her husband collected throughout their life, archaeology, and books that have no place on the shelves of children. She has gone mad and speaks now of how lilac-colored ink has the best smell of them all, pausing from time to time to mention the ridiculousness of a life in which you gather more than you become and gasp for air. Her apartment is still packed with books, every time you move your feet you step on something, a book, a statue, a record, a memory—anamnesis. When her health declined and her mind vanished completely inside the photographs of her and Boris—young, holding hands, clutching books, visiting the world—she gave in to the wishes of her family to sell the apartment and move back north.

Silvia left Bucharest in a wheelchair, drugged, lied to, despised by her neighbors for ruining the harmony of their flawlessly crafted lives in communist buildings. She left Bucharest as a burden, even on the shoulders of strangers passing by. I remember that day perfectly. Everyone was gathered outside, cheering for her departure, longing to finally be rid of mad Silvia, of her books that smelled like death and malodorous plaster, of her liqueur breath bothering everyone as she was reaching to say goodbye. The image of my mother's hand grabbing my wrist as I was leaning in to kiss Silvia one last time will never leave me. I have carried it with me through all the moments of my life when, whether out of fear or comfort, I avoided taking steps towards what I longed for.

I did kiss her one last time, for when my mother grabbed my wrist, her eyes met Silvia's and she once again saw the woman who kept me warm and safe in the afternoon all those years, and she let go of my hand. Silvia left Bucharest barely able to utter a word, her cold hands gripping on to the spine of two museum books with her name on the covers and the photograph of young Boris smiling at her in sepia tones still pinned to her bathrobe. She left reaching for my hands one last time. She gave me an ashtray carved out from an old stone her and Boris found on one of their excavating adventures. I grabbed it and promised to write her story.

The following thought could have been found by a film-maker thirty kilometers outside of Paris. Fossils posing as silver fabrics that embrace the cynicism of homesickness and all that comes with it. Smoke from a bonfire by the river. What becomes of our joys and sufferings if life on Earth is merely a found footage on the outskirts of a cliché? I am standing at a crossroad, pen in hand, mapping the world on the inside of my arms, like children from merry-go-round dreams used to do. All my voices are bound to different names, at different times, in different places. I am standing in decline, in flight, in retreat. To have a body is to be visible.

I once met a man who used to draw little black hearts on the cheeks of graveyard sculptures. He told me stories about angels removing photographs of our diseased naked bodies from waiting rooms, morgues, and chapels. "Flesh is sinful," he would whisper to himself in the coldness of funereal mornings. He told me stories about the nobility of looking out for each other when we pass through a door that is foreign to us. He called them portals—I called them moments. Moments to help me breathe. Moments to help me remember. Moments to point to a novel path. *Moments* to relieve pain. He told me stories about protecting one another with words and phrases, nestled safely in beds of punctuation and regress. I would listen while drawing chalk lines between myself and the world, while moving from one corner of the room to the other—from the theater to the cinema, from the beach to the university basement, from the stairs of Montmartre to the bridges of Budapest. He told me stories and I listened, pretending he was the grandfather I never knew on my father's side.

Sequences from all the places I lived in come to me in juxtapositions of snow and crimson-red hunger. Lace curtains blown by the wind. The smell of paraffin, dust, and days of infancy lingers into the sequence of memories now so altered that I no longer allow myself to call my own. A still of a book resting open upon a gray metal table comes to mind. The house at the edge of the forest, always in danger of being flooded by the river where preventorium children played in the sand. The weightlessness of hunger and shame. My fragments perish at various times and in different places. I will die and find myself as fossils embedded on the site of someone's memory—marginalia on the shelf of a stranger, a footnote in the history of my ancestors. An unclothed body, decaying under the shelter of soil, lingering on the possibility of still being sensitive to nature, light, and color in the afterworld. Sequences of wax figures, dreams, and trees snapping in the night, interpose with the ones from earlier. When we no longer speak of belonging, we start to see ourselves dispassionately. We see ourselves in the layers of others—as the layers of others. I see myself from afar, passing through the home of the dying. At times, I see myself as the cluster of possibilities I once was. I see myself respecting the rites of passage but longing for something else altogether. I see the physical milieu of an undefeated night in the fading colors of doors from other lives, other hearts, other poems, other wounds.

Mikhail Bakhtin wrote that where there is no passing of time, there is also no moment of time. Things take longer to happen during traumatic episodes, they become a long dream—a never-ending dream. The space between two people expands to the point of eternity. Not the distance, not the closeness, but the space that was once just right—the space that for some reason, no one ever notices. When you write of trauma, the space between two people becomes the space between two words. A space that is no longer needed, yet a space we strive to rediscover. We do not need its language but we use it to tell our story. I no longer crave pauses, distance, blank pages, I no longer crave the words that described the world as paradise. From film frame to film frame, I do not remember the space in between. From body to body, I do not touch the space in between. From smile to smile, I do not breathe the space in between. It happens here, in the width between two words, in the space between two people. Passing through the home of the dying. Passing through the green door, the red door—passing through the blue door, resting not on the small bed, not on the larger one by the window, but on the floor, surrounded by books, silk ribbons, and memories of going mussel hunting. The chronotope becomes a force—tachypsychia takes on the form of a memory error.

Some twenty years later, I am living in a ruined apartment. My skin smells of honey and linden blossoms. I have reproductions of Evelyn de Morgan's paintings all over the place. Her *Life and Thought Emerging from the Tomb* is the first thing I see when walking through the door. Trauma lives in the body of all things—past, present, and future. Taut and sharp, as blood on the demise of the individual. *Night and Sleep* is a bookmark in one of my phenomenology readings. A cozy life in a nice flat, with letters instead of numbers on the colorless door. I live untroubled by violence, nudity, or the smell of warm gingerbread that crumbles in your mouth on winter nights. *Cadmus and Harmonia* adorns the bedroom floor. I became a monothematic film character, I allowed myself to be pushed into the background, to be abandoned on the cutting-room floor. Almost somebody. *Ariadne in Naxos* sits contemptuously on the living room wall. Blue cigarettes remind me of the cerulean door that opened my old room in the village. A late-night train passes and its vibration shakes the memory from my mind, replacing it with that of starving trains becoming one with the canopy of the forest. *Lux in Tenebris* on the balcony, keeping company to a dead plant and books stained by raindrops and the afterthought of *Demeter Mourning for Persephone*. To be absent from the body is to be absent from all bodies. To never be entirely anywhere. I close my eyes and think of all the places I called *home*, wondering if I was ever truly present in any of them. I close my eyes and wonder if home was ever a place. I was never entirely present in that apartment, I never felt present. My existence within the confines of that space faded long before I ever decided to leave it—even though, from time to time, my mind lingers on the cozy evenings I spent alone, reading, writing, drafting forthcoming paths. The only memory I have of abandoning it is a weaving of a lipstick trace on an empty glass in the hallway by the broken mirror, the shape of a painting I no longer recall the name of, and the creaking sound made by the colorless door as I closed it behind me.

It never gets dark. I am revisiting pages on healing and the trauma of the skin under an unfamiliar light. Pages on texture, conjunction, embodiment, emotional experience—after which I write. I write on my flesh about the possibility of the mountain becoming the possibility of the sea. I reach for the light—not to possess it, but to extinguish it. I reach too often, I reach too keenly, I reach too deeply. Other words speak to me of surface sensitivity, cutaneous contact, touch, smell, taste. I need to be held. I need to be rocked, choked—reassured. I need to be bruised, blindfolded, caressed. I need to become the force of the surface, of any surface—for I need to be able to reach, still.

Existence is corporeal. Flesh and blood—blending, belonging, overlapping, meeting, corresponding with my being. With the nail and the hole, with shadows behind my eyelids. I close my eyes and as I touch my skin, I realize that my armor has yet again hardened. Even with my eyes closed, through the subtle play of lighting in the room, I am able to make out further layers of texture. I fold, I reject, I read—I silence the pen. I feel intimately connected to something, to words encrusted on the living; to attitude, gestures, movement. I am intimately connected to lust, to tyranny, to machines. My hands touch each other in remembrance of all the things they have gathered—in remembrance of time passing, of maladies, of healing. My hands touch each other, my fingers intertwine, and I long for stories I have not yet written. I tell time by touching walls, nails, holes, other bodies. Yet again incapable of sensing, I rely on touch to find the residual parts of my form. I think of words then I stitch them together on the skin of those around me. I am never alone. It never gets dark. I am unrecognizable. Monstrous. Distorted. I reach too keenly for the light I need to extinguish. For the story, for its creator, for the bearer of darkness. There are no keys; there is no imprisonment. Focused not on dreams but on my everyday reality, I reassure myself by no longer reading the papers. Instead, I use them to light fires perhaps hoping their flames would be able to engulf the light. The relationship I have with fire changes once more. I close my eyes and touch something. I feel the brick wall crushing the layers of my skin. There is no beginning, and there is no end.

I walk aimlessly, caressing the curtain of an imaginary rain, talking to myself, searching through the darkness for a flicker of light—I am hollow and yet I know that there is no room inside me for anything else than the silence and quietness of unborn selves. I rest eternally inside the carcass of the world, burdened by the weight of my fingers interlocking, humbled by the sweat on my forehead as the shadow of the forest shelters me under poplar sighs. I wound and I am wounded—my hair wet and heavy from the rain, the steps of my thoughts coming from so far away. I bury my flesh at the feet of the gate that never opened. As the wind carries farther and farther the alms that were placed on my slab, I rest within the carcass of the world—absent, with interlocking fingers that move from time to time, sending a call to the wild beasts that otherwise would not dare to interrupt my slumber. I am the eye of an unforgiving goddess, watching over creatures walking aimlessly through an imaginary rain.

I spend most of my time thinking about excess and its philosophical merits. About the lack of measure, about obsession as a constructive form of the self and what it does to our bodies. In my fondness for the extreme, I regard excess as an *a priori grandeur* enabling all other experiences. As the most beautiful tree in the forest. When I long for coldness, I take photographs of city statues and compare them to those of autumn leaves. It helps me understand the proximity of excess—yet there are no signs of forthcoming devastation around me. The ruins are already here. Excess becoming excessive is not a concern that occupies my mind. Like the majority of those whom I have read with devotion throughout my life, I see excess as a fundamental attitude, a consistent trait of human nature. I welcome the voluptuousness of inner conflict. I search to uproot myself. I search for meaning from a state of limbo, gasping for reason, being engulfed by bitterness while methodically examining the sordidness of reality in the creases of the flesh. Existence is always corporeal. The debris we gather along the way is corporeal, our bodies are the vessels of our memories, experiences, thoughts, and touches. The fossil assemblage brought together by veins rushing like water currents is corporeal as long as our bodies survive. For only a living body can transport its history to the place of its posthumous discovery. Our living moments—fossils and bones deposited by a predator on a land that only becomes familiar in death.

To write of the self is to plunge your fingers deep into the rivers that carry fossils, memories, animal bones, desecrated flesh, ashes, thorns, trauma—to dive into the collection of lifeforms that your body and mind have gathered along the way. To retrace and extract with implausible precision the very things that you wanted buried, in an attempt to sketch a beginning and an end—the lines of a personal history, blended together in a manner satisfactory enough to let into the light. In philosophy, *anamnesis* belongs to Plato. In medicine, it belongs to the patient. For the rest of the world, it is merely a recollection of things past. Our history is a poem we get to reword over and over again—bending time, redefining moments, healing wounds, being gentle with our scars and the scars of others. A poem that is both deeply personal and universal, its lines taking the shape of stories we pour on ourselves and into the hearts of those around us. A poem we write time and time again, whether we are quarantined in the ruins or reclining in the light. To write of the self is to be seduced by every anomaly, to bend it to our will and liking; it is to rebel against all truths. To write of the self is to write of touches drenched in the departure of an imaginary fall, at the edge of a fictitious forest, alongside mythological bodies of water, under trees that lose their leaves during the day and blossom at night in dreams—to write of dirt that throbs in burdening harmony with raindrops and rushing footsteps. To write of the self is to melt away into wet cement. To call upon your body for renewal, to plead and beg and kneel for it to provide you with a new set of cells—untouched skin.

In retracing the origins of *melancholy*, Marsilio Ficino's *De Vita Libri Tres* contains a passage in which he discusses the effects of love on the body and soul of lovers. Ficino writes about how relentlessly turning our thoughts in the direction of our beloved causes the body to wither and dry out, it causes the blood to blacken and eventually give birth to melancholy. A continuous recollection of the same person, object, or emotion, threatening the health of those who engage in it—a motif that is widely spread throughout literature, philosophy, and science. Fixation, obsession, the throbbing of one's arteries due to the same *object of desire*, carving one's passions in the same stone, time and time again, until the body withers and the blood blackens. To write of the self is to turn all thought inwards—towards the inside, the mind, the spirit, the organs—to shed light on the cave-dwelling fish. As in the case of love, the process can only be understood and embraced through self-reflection and personal experiences.

The first written words that made an impression on me were not on paper—in fact, they were not words at all, but stick figures on freshly-painted walls. I was three years old, sitting on the floor of the main room. As I was dismantling the parts of a model train, my grandmother walked into the room holding a small bowl of ink. She took my hands, bathed them in the cobalt liquid, and encouraged me to write on the walls. I drew stick figures instead, but as years passed, as my mind gathered more experiences and created an ampler context, those lines and circles took the shape of the first poem I ever wrote.

We engage with images from the exterior world with each breath we take—images that demand our attention and petition our nervous system. When our nerves are damaged, when the signal gets disrupted, the manner in which we perceive those images becomes distorted or even erased. When excitement no longer reaches our brain, when the currents of touch no longer travel through our epidermis, when the trembling of nerves is no longer operational to our body's processes and mechanisms, the exterior world is no longer needed. Henri Bergson described perception not only as reality of the mind but also as part of the exterior reality—perception is not in us, but in the objects we perceive. Traveling the corners of my mind in search for just enough to build a biography, I found myself re-examining several periods and places more than once, distorting the image I had of them with each visit. In doing so, I inadvertently reburied instances that perhaps should have been brought back to life—experiences that have shaped and guided me, that have injured and healed me beyond recognition. A phenomenon which I find peculiar, because I know with certitude that I do not want them to get lost, that I do not want them to be abandoned in the wreckage so that they cannot be extracted before eternally embedding themselves into the site of discovery.

The precarious study of being, *becoming* and *existing* did not leave prominent marks upon my ability to understand myself. It did not stop me from incorporating mythology, fairy tales, and the histories of others into myself. It did not stop me from seeing myth as a sort of metaphysical memory—something to hold onto when struggling to release myself from the chain of chronological events that enslaved me. By one path or another, sometimes breathing just enough to keep the blood circulating, I have discovered that physical pain and pain of the mind are bound up with the most fundamental questions about the self, for if I were to not feel any pain, I would not crave to articulate a remedy through the incessant nature of writing; to prise apart that which makes and unmakes us.

Illiquid, bereft, and unearthed, I hunger to catch all minutes—to postpone the moment when we will disappear with them into the trees. The moment when unrolling the spool of thread will plunge me back into the center of my inner labyrinth. Digging through all that crafts my identity, I rarely search for the things that help me sleep at night. I do not stumble upon the gentle things, the light things that travel the body in a tender manner—sometimes not leaving any trace, other times offering precisely what is needed. I do not linger upon their surface, for I know those are not the things that have shaped me—they are not the things that have birthed my hunger for writing. Just as objects, bodies, and processes of nature are made of matter, and that matter gives them the possibility to take on a shape of their own, so writing too takes a shape of its own—a shape malleable in itself yet seldom manipulated by exterior factors. Thus, to write of the self is to understand and come to terms with the fact that even when the book is finished, the ink does not dry out and the page does not stop gifting nor does it stop consuming. To write of the self is to write not the story of one's journey through the labyrinth—it is to write the labyrinth itself. To write of the self is to write in the shape of a wound that never stops opening.

ACKNOWLEDGMENTS

Earlier versions of several chapters and passages appeared in the following publications: "Carrying Within Me Another Time" in *Uncolonized* (Zeno Press), "With Hair of the Wolf" in *Reliquiae* (Corbel Stone Press), "Sensorium" in Sublunary Editions, "Passing Through the Home of the Dying" and "As We Extend to More Than Just Our Bodies" in Burning House Press, and "A Biographical Accident" in minor literature[s].

I would like to thank the editors of these publications for their support.

CHRISTINA TUDOR-SIDERI is a writer and translator living in Eastern Europe. Her work deals with the absent body and its anonymous rhythms, myth, memory, narrative deferral, and the imprisonment of the mind within the time and space of its corporeal vessel.

Sublunary Editions is a small, independent press based in Seattle, Washington. Founded by Joshua Rothes in 2019, it publishes short books of innovative writing from a world-wide cadre of authors. Subscriptions are available at:
<u>subeds.com/subscribe</u>

OTHER SUBLUNARY EDITIONS TITLES

Falstaff: Apotheosis
Pierre Senges (translated by Jacob Siefring)

926 Years
Kyle Coma-Thompson, Tristan Foster

Corpses
Vik Shirley

A Luminous History of the Palm
Jessica Sequeira

The Wreck of the Large Glass / Paleódromo
Mónica Belevan